NELSON MANDELA
Fighting to Dismantle Apartheid

NELSON MANDELA
Fighting to Dismantle Apartheid

Ann Malaspina

Enslow Publishing
101 W. 23rd Street
Suite 240
New York, NY 10011
USA
enslow.com

Published in 2018 by Enslow Publishing, LLC.
101 W. 23rd Street, Suite 240, New York, NY 10011

Library of Congress Cataloging-in-Publication Data

Names: Malaspina, Ann, 1957–author.
Title: Nelson Mandela : fighting to dismantle apartheid / Ann Malaspina.
Other titles: Rebels with a cause.
Description: New York, NY : Enslow Publishing, 2018. | Series: Rebels with a
  cause | Includes bibliographical references and index. | Audience: Grades
  7-12.
Identifiers: LCCN 2017003085| ISBN 9780766085176 (library-bound)
Subjects: LCSH: Mandela, Nelson, 1918-2013—Juvenile literature. | Political
  activists—South Africa—Biography—Juvenile literature. | Blacks—Civil
  rights—South Africa–Juvenile literature. | Apartheid—South
  Africa—History–Juvenile literature. | Civil rights movements—South
  Africa—History–20th century—Juvenile literature. | South Africa—Race
  relations—History—20th century—Juvenile literature.
Classification: LCC DT1974 .M283 2017 | DDC 968.07/1092 [B]—dc23
LC record available at https://lccn.loc.gov/2017003085

Printed in the United States of America

To Our Readers: We have done our best to make sure all website addresses in this book were active and appropriate when we went to press. However, the author and the publisher have no control over and assume no liability for the material available on those websites or on any websites they may link to. Any comments or suggestions can be sent by email to customerservice@enslow.com.

CONTENTS

INTRODUCTION

The tall man with broad shoulders stood in the dock at the front of the courtroom. Charged with sabotage and conspiracy to overthrow the government of South Africa, Nelson Mandela faced the ultimate penalty, death by hanging. For over a year, the prosecution in the so-called Rivonia Trial had argued its case against him and his codefendants. The men were antiapartheid fighters who had been trying to overturn the oppressive racial regime of South Africa. On April 20, 1964, the defense team began its case, and Mandela at last had a chance to speak. "I am the first accused," he began.[1]

Mandela, a forty-five-year-old lawyer and political activist, had spent over ten days writing the statement by hand in his jail cell. He had read the statement aloud to his fellow accused and to his lawyers and supporters. One commented that Mandela would be hung if he read the statement in court. Others begged him not to go forward. But Mandela was determined to tell the world why he was willing to risk his freedom, and even his life, to battle apartheid.

Nelson Mandela, shown here in 1960, spent much of his life battling the oppression and injustice of the apartheid system in South Africa.

The system of apartheid, in place since 1948, had stripped South Africa's majority nonwhite population of its basic rights of citizenship. Blacks, Indians, and "coloureds," the South African term for people of mixed race, could not vote or choose where to live. Forced to carry passes and relegated to segregated, crowded townships and low-paying jobs, they had endured generations of poverty and endless indignities, while South Africa's white minority ran the government and held the economic reigns. Yet thus far, there had been little anyone could do to change the status quo. Apartheid was supported by laws and imposed by force. Those who defied the system risked imprisonment or even worse.

Like the water fountains, classrooms, and buses of South Africa, the seating in the ornate courtroom in the grand Palace of Justice in Pretoria was segregated by race. Whites sat on one side of the room, and blacks on the other. All were quiet as Mandela launched into his statement that combined confession and defiance.

Mandela did not deny that he had planned sabotage against the government. Unlike other famous rebel leaders, such as Mohandas K. Gandhi and the Reverend Martin Luther King Jr., who believed that justice could be won by nonviolence, Mandela had turned to force to fight for freedom after trying many alternatives. He told the court, "I did not plan it in a spirit of recklessness nor because I have any love of violence. I planned it as a result of a calm and sober assessment of the political situation that had arisen after many years of tyranny, exploitation, and oppression of my people by whites."[2] As his statement revealed, Mandela's strongest weapon was not violence but words. People listened when he spoke. They remembered what he said.

Outside in the streets, people held up signs and called out for the defendants' release. But inside the courtroom, Mandela heard only his own voice. "During my lifetime I have devoted myself to the struggle of the African people," he said. "I have fought against white domination, and I have fought against black domination. I have cherished the ideal of a democratic and free society in which all persons live together in harmony and with equal opportunities. It is an ideal which I hope to live for and to achieve. But if needs be, it is an ideal for which I am prepared to die."[3]

The Rivonia Trial came to an end. On June 11, 1964, Mandela was found guilty on charges of sabotage and conspiracy. He was sentenced to life imprisonment. For nearly twenty-seven years, he would be confined to prison and absent from public view. As the years passed, Mandela's voice, even in captivity, would grow stronger. From the confines of his prison cell, Mandela's determination to bring human dignity and civil rights to all South Africans would burn brighter, until it was impossible to ignore. In the streets of London, the halls of the United Nations (UN), and the alleys of Soweto, the cry "Free Nelson Mandela!" would rise to a deafening roar. It was a demand for not just one man's freedom, but an entire people's.

1

Son of Royalty

Nelson Mandela was born on July 18, 1918, in the village of Mevso in the remote southeastern region of South Africa known as the Transkei. Set on the banks of the Mbashe River, the village was surrounded by green hills, where cattle and sheep grazed and farmers planted maize. Mandela was a Xhosa, one of South Africa's largest ethnic groups. The Xhosa had fished, hunted, and lived in the Transkei for many generations. The Xhosa people are divided into tribes, and Mandela's great-grandfather, Ngubengcuka, was the great king of the Thembu tribe.

Mandela's father, Nkosi Mphakanyiswa Gadla Mandela, known as Hendry, was the chief of Mevso and the principal advisor to the acting Thembu king or chief. Mandela's mother, Nonqaphi Nosekeni, known as Fanny, was the third of Hendry's four wives. The practice of having four wives was expected for Xhosa chiefs. Mandela was one of his father's thirteen children and the youngest of four sons. He considered his father's other three wives his mothers, and his stepbrothers and stepsisters his siblings. Later in his life, Mandela spoke warmly of his large family that provided him with love and a sense of belonging.

Goats graze outside a rondavel, a traditional mud house in the Transkei, similar to Mandela's childhood home.

The Mandela family was respected, and the new baby was welcomed as royalty. Mandela's parents named him Rolihlahla, meaning "pulling the branch of a tree" or "troublemaker" in the Xhosa language. Xhosa people also belong to clans. As an adult, Mandela liked to be called Madiba, his clan name.

Despite their social standing, the Mandelas, like all South Africans, lived under the rules of a white colonial government. In 1910, the Union of South Africa had been established, bringing the country into the fold of the British monarchy. When Mandela was still a baby, his father defied the orders of the local British judge. He lost his position, as well as his land, cattle, and other possessions. As a result, the family had to move to Qunu, a smaller village accessible only by grassy paths.

In Qunu, each wife had her own *kraal*, a group of huts with a pen for animals and a field to plant vegetables. Mandela's mother had three *rondavels*, or mud huts, for sleeping, cooking, and storing food. There were no beds or tables. The family slept on mats and ate on the ground from a single dish. In the village, the boys took care of the animals, and the girls and women ground the maize and cooked meals in metal pots over the fire.

By age five, Mandela was herding cattle and sheep with a switch, gathering wild honey and fruit, swimming in the streams, and catching fish with twine. He also learned to stick fight, a traditional children's game. The young players held sticks in both hands and tried to avoid

TRADITIONAL XHOSA ARCHITECTURE

In the grassy hills of Eastern Cape Province, the traditional Xhosa rondavel provide housing for many people. The walls are made of local mud, and the roofs from thatched grasses. The floors are packed with dirt. The rondavels, which are usually round, have a single room, lit by the sunlight through the doorway. Each rondavel has a purpose—for sleeping, cooking, or storage space. Families like Nelson Mandela's had several rondavels grouped together in a kraal.

blows and escape opponents. Mandela's sharp senses and quick feet made him a champion.

Mandela's childhood in a Xhosa village gave him roots and a strong identity. From his father, he learned that the colonial government might take away a job but not a person's pride. He saw that his father had "a proud rebelliousness, a stubborn sense of fairness."[1] Those were qualities that Mandela would try to emulate. But the world was changing, and Mandela could not take the same path as his father. Already, South Africa had begun to harden its discrimination against black Africans. The Natives Land Act of 1913 prohibited them from buying land or sharecropping in 93 percent of the country.[2] Forbidden from owning land in white areas, many lost their ancestral land and their livelihoods.

> **"In my youth in the Transkei I listened to the elders of my tribe telling stories of the old days. Amongst the tales they related to me were those of wars fought by our ancestors in defence of the fatherland. The names of Dingane and Bambata, Hintsa and Makana, Squngthi and Dalasile."[3]**

In more personal ways, the world was also changing for Mandela and the Xhosa people. Protestantism, spread by British missionaries, was replacing the traditional Xhosa religion. Mandela's mother had converted to Christianity and baptized Mandela as a Methodist. Missionary schools provided a British education to children in rural villages like Qunu. Neither of his parents could read or write, but in modern South Africa, a child needed an education.

The Mandelas were determined that their son would have the best one possible.

A New Name

On his first day of school, seven-year-old Mandela took off the traditional Xhosa blanket that he wore every day. His father gave him a pair of his own trousers, cut at the knee and tied at the waist with a piece of string. In the single-room Methodist schoolhouse, Mandela met his teacher, Miss Mdingane. Right away, she gave him the British name Nelson. His African name Rolihlahla did not matter to the teacher, nor did his identity as Xhosa royalty. "There was no such thing as African culture," he wrote later.[4] From then on, he was known as Nelson.

More changes were coming. When Mandela was around twelve years old, his father fell ill. Believing death was near, Hendry turned to his cousin Jongintaba Dalindyebo, who was the acting regent, or leader, of the Thembu tribe. He asked Jongintaba to take care of his son. After Hendry's death, his mother took him on foot to the royal palace of the Thembu, known as the Great Place, at Mqhekezweni. The settlement had a school, church, a large house, and many huts. For Mandela, who carried a tin trunk and whose hand-me-down pants were still tied with a string, his new surroundings seemed exciting.

He joined the regent's family and grew close to his cousin Justice. Jongintaba was an important man. From miles around, Thembus came to him for favors and advice. Jongintaba told Mandela that a leader is like a shepherd who has to persuade the sheep to stay with the flock. By observing Jongintaba and other elders, Mandela learned Xhosa values such as *ubuntu*, or human brotherhood, which emphasizes compassion, gentleness, hospitality, and support for others.

Mandela also learned about the Xhosa's democratic government, with its traditions of debate and compromise. Those ideals would stay with him. But the Xhosas were suffering under colonization. Wars with the British had pushed out many of the Xhosa chiefs, and land had been lost. Even so, stories of his ancestors, particularly his great-grandfather, the Thembu king, left deep impressions on Mandela. "I knew that our society had produced black heroes and this filled me with pride," he wrote.[5]

Traditional Ceremony

At sixteen, Mandela underwent the traditional Thembu ceremony to become a man. Along with twenty-four other boys, he traveled to a valley on a river and lived in a simple lodge. The boys had to bathe at dawn in the river and then undergo circumcision. After the uncomfortable event was over, Mandela was able to declare, "Ndiyindoda!" This is the Xhosa word for "I am a man." Mandela was also given the name Dalibunga, meaning "founder of the Bunga," which was the body that ruled the Transkei.[6] He was a man now, able to marry, own land, and make his way in the world.

The regent was training Mandela to become the advisor to the king of the Thembus. For that role, Mandela needed a top-notch education. In 1934, he was sent to Clarkebury, a Methodist boarding school with a reputation for educating promising students. In fact, the school was founded with the help of Mandela's great-grandfather, who had befriended a Methodist missionary. Clarkebury emphasized European culture and the English language.

Mandela's tribal status held little sway. At school, Mandela gained a deep respect for reading and learning.

Two years later, he was sent to Healdtown, a larger British Methodist school. Students had to wear jackets and maroon-and-gold ties and sing the British anthem, "God Save the King." They studied British history and literature. The lessons reminded Mandela that the Xhosa were beaten by the British colonists. A few black teachers taught African history and other subjects. Mandela won a prize for an essay he wrote on the Xhosa in 1938. After he graduated that same year, Mandela went on to university with his cousin Justice.

University

The South African Native College at Fort Hare was the only black university in the country. The university educated the sons of royal and wealthy families. The student body also included a few whites, Indians, and coloureds. Though Mandela didn't know it at the time, the college's bright students would become "a seedbed of the revolution" to overturn white rule in South Africa.[7]

Mandela was twenty-one years old when he entered university. Some of his new friends, including a young man named Oliver Tambo, were active in politics. At first, Mandela was not interested; he set his mind on becoming a court interpreter, a secure civil service job that was respected by the Xhosas, but his mind soon changed.

Standing Up to Power

Mandela's first taste of political action came when students became upset at the food in the dining room. He

Mandela wears boxing gloves in 1952. As a boxer, he was confident and light on his feet, but not strong or fast enough to fight professionally. Instead, Mandela sparred in anti-apartheid battles and politics

was elected to the Students' Representative Council and began to demand better food. The principal of the school ordered new elections to oust the council members. Most of the students boycotted the vote, and Mandela stepped down from the council. Angry at Mandela's insubordination, the principal expelled him, and he and Justice returned home. For the first time, Mandela stood up to power and accepted the consequences. It wouldn't be the last.

Back home, the regent urged Mandela and Justice to go back to school, but they refused. Shortly after, the regent chose brides for the two young men. Mandela wanted nothing to do with an arranged marriage. He and Justice decided to run away to Johannesburg. By defying the regent, Mandela threw away both his education and his security, at least for now. In exchange, he opened the doors to a life built on his own terms.

2

Cradle of Humankind

As Mandela struggled to find his life's path, South Africa was searching for its own future. Wars, invasions, and civil strife between racial and ethnic groups had confronted the region for as long as anyone alive could remember. Before it could become a

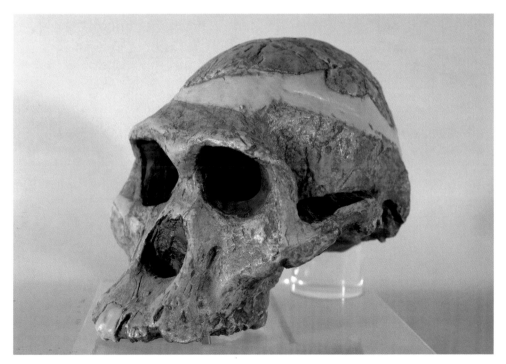

This is a reproduction of the skull of the adult *Australopithicus afracanus* fossil found in the limestone caves of Sterkontein, South Africa.

modern nation, South Africa would have to free itself from its past.

For much of its history, the medium-sized country at the southern tip of the African continent was isolated from the world. Encompassing 471,400 square miles (1,220,920 square kilometers), or about one-eighth the area of the United States, South Africa is bounded on the west by the Atlantic Ocean and the east by the Indian Ocean. Strong ocean currents and summer and winter gales kept ships away from its rocky shores. The difficulties of travel across the African continent discouraged migration.

A vast plateau, a high flat area made of old rock, covers most of South Africa. Some of the plateau is grasslands, known as the Highveld. The tree-covered plains are called the Bushveld. Elephants, lions, giraffes, zebras, hippopotamuses, and antelope roam the grasslands and plains. Surrounding the plateau on the east, south, and west is the Great Escarpment, a jagged mountainous region with some peaks higher than 11,400 feet (3,474 meters). The country's rivers drain in the dry season, so the water can't be used for trade or travel during this time. Along the coast are few natural harbors, but also rain forests and sandy beaches.

Despite its geography and a climate wracked by droughts, South Africa harbored some of the earliest human life. Fossils of early ancestors of modern humans have been found in several sites. In the Sterkfontein limestone caves in the grasslands between Johannesburg and Pretoria, Scottish paleoanthropologist Dr. Robert Broom discovered the fossil remains of an *Australopithecus africanus*, who lived approximately 2.5 million years ago.[1] The complete skull, missing only its teeth, was named Mrs. Ples. The limestone caves, with many important fossil discoveries, are preserved in the Cradle of Humankind World Heritage Site.

By 100,000 BCE, tribes of hunter-gatherers known as the San or the Bushmen had moved into South Africa around the Kalahari Desert in the Northwest. They are considered the first human inhabitants of South Africa. They used stones for tools. In about 500 CE, people speaking Bantu languages migrated from central and eastern Africa. They began to herd sheep and cattle about two thousand years ago. Later, around 200 CE, they planted crops and raised livestock, and iron tools were introduced.

In the 1400s, the Bantu-speaking Zulu and Xhosa peoples formed large kingdoms with distinctive languages and cultures. The Zulu, traditionally grain farmers and cattle herders, are the largest ethnic group in South Africa. The Xhosa, Mandela's people, are the second largest. But the Zulu, Xhosa, and other indigenous South Africans would soon become imperiled.

Fort and Garden

By the end of the fifteenth century, the age of exploration was underway. Portuguese explorers Bartolomeu Dias and Vasco da Gama sailed in separate voyages around the Cape of Good Hope, the rocky headland at the tip of South Africa, in the late 1400s. They are thought to be the first Europeans to encounter the region. It was only a matter of time before Europeans staked their claims on the ancient land.

In 1652, the Dutch captain Jan van Riebeeck and his crew of ninety men landed at the Cape of Good Hope. They were sent by the Dutch East India Company to build a fort and plant a garden for ships on the trade route. The settlement became Cape Town, one of modern South Africa's three capital cities. Dutch farmers built houses and raised crops. They called themselves Boers, the Dutch word for "farmer." Some Boers took Africans as slaves.

French and British settlers soon sought footholds in the region. Wars in Europe heightened the struggle to dominate the strategic tip of Africa. In 1806, the British won control of Cape Town. By 1820, thousands of British settlers were arriving to seek new lives in Africa. Pushed out of the area, the Dutch moved inland, a journey known as the Great Trek. They fought the Zulu and won at the Battle of Blood River in 1838. Some three thousand Zulu warriors were killed. The Boers founded the republics of the Transvaal in 1852 and the Orange Free State in 1854.

The European colonists wreaked havoc on the Africans. Smallpox and other diseases killed whole villages. Wars

SLAVE ECONOMY

The early years of the Cape Colony settlement, the Dutch established an economy based on slavery. The slaves came from far and wide—Indonesia, India, Ceylon, as well as parts of Africa. By 1793, there were nearly fifteen thousand slaves who worked as servants, fishers, gardeners, artisans, and farm laborers.[2] The slaves had few rights. They were not allowed to marry, acquire property, or leave wills. They had to follow all orders and were threatened by violence if they disobeyed.

stole Africans' lands and security. The slaveholding of the Boers planted the seeds for the apartheid system that Mandela would later fight to overturn. However, the British in the 1830s began freeing the slaves in their territories.

Diamonds and Gold

In the winter of 1866 to 1867, a Boer teenager named Erasmus Jacobs found an unusual rock on his father's farm along the Orange River. The rock turned out to be a diamond—and the discovery shook the world. The town

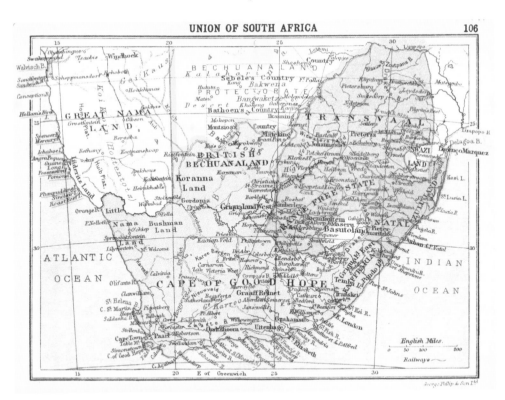

The Union of South Africa united the Cape Colony, Natal, the Transvaal, and the Orange Free State, as shown in a 1912 map.

of Kimberly, which became part of the Cape Colony in 1880, was the center of the diamond-mining industry. The railroad arrived in Kimberly to carry the diamonds to the world in 1885.

With cheap black labor, diamond production skyrocketed. Two British immigrants, Cecil Rhodes and Barney Barnato, became fierce rivals as their mining and holding companies grew. Dependent on black labor, they each vied to earn the most riches. South Africa remains a major diamond producer today.

South Africa's ground held other valuable minerals. In 1886, two prospectors discovered a gold reef on the Langlaagte farm in the Transvaal. People began digging

CECIL RHODES

Cecil Rhodes (1852–1902), the controversial British entrepreneur, mine owner, and politician, built an empire in South Africa that relied on cheap black labor and the subjugation of black people. As prime minister of the Cape Colony from 1890 to 1896, he enacted many racist policies that would pave the way to apartheid. He once said, "I contend that we are the first race in the world, and that the more of the world we inhabit the better it is for the human race."[4] After his death, he left much of his fortune to the Rhodes Scholarships program. Every year, talented young people of all races from around the world receive scholarships to study at Oxford University.

on other farms south of Pretoria. People flocked to find quick riches, and Johannesburg was established as a small village and, later, the largest city in South Africa. Rhodes's company, Gold Fields of South Africa, operated the largest mines. Rhodes later served as prime minister of the Cape Colony. He was a strong advocate of white rule of Africa. "We must find new lands from which we can easily obtain raw materials and at the same time exploit the cheap slave labor that is available from the natives of the colonies," said Rhodes.[3]

Racially based labor laws that allowed only whites to holds clerical and professional jobs forced many black men into the mines. In the next decades, tens of thousands of men flocked to the mines. They lived in crowded dormitories far from home and worked long hours, often underground, for very low wages and with few health and safety protections.

Union of South Africa

The discovery of minerals made South Africa more alluring to Europeans. In turn, the promise of wealth created tension among the colonists who wanted control of South Africa. In 1899, a major war broke out between the British Empire and the Boer's South African Republic, or Transvaal, and the Orange Free State. In the fierce conflict, known as the South African War, the Boers used guerrilla tactics to battle the British troops. The British gathered Boer women and children into camps, where tens of thousands died of disease.

In 1902, the Boers were defeated and the two sides signed the Peace of Vereeniging. The British gave the Boers amnesty and took over their lands. In 1910, the

THE RHODES COLOSSUS
STRIDING FROM CAPE TOWN TO CAIRO.

British entrepreneur Cecil Rhodes is shown walking across Africa from Cape Town to Cairo with a telegraph wire in this December 10, 1892 cartoon from *Punch* magazine.

British established the Union of South Africa, made up of four provinces: the Transvaal and Orange Free State, formerly Boer republics, and Natal and the Cape Colony, once British colonies. The Union of South Africa was part of the British Empire. The British monarch was represented in the government by a governor-general, and the congress was led by a prime minister. The first prime minister was Louis Botha, a Boer army general.

The population of the new country was imbalanced. It consisted of four million blacks, 1,275,000 whites, 500,000 coloureds, and 150,000 Indians.[5] The new constitution gave all political power to the small white minority. They already held the economic power. Even before the South African War, racial laws had been enforced. For instance, the General Pass Regulations Bill of 1905 denied blacks the vote, forced them to stay in certain areas, and required them to carry identity cards. The new government enacted more racial laws. The Mine and Works Act of 1911 allowed only whites and coloureds to gain certification for skilled labor in the mines. The Natives Land Act of 1913 prohibited blacks from living and farming on most land. The Natives Act of 1923 forced blacks to live on the outskirts of cities, away from white neighborhoods, and have work contracts in order to even live there.[6] These laws not only kept blacks from opportunity and freedom but also bolstered poorer whites, including the Boer farmers.

African National Congress

South Africa's blacks needed a political voice. Yet they were scattered in rural villages and big cities, spoke different languages, and belonged to different tribes. Some had been educated in the missionary schools and abroad. Others did not read or write. To gain influence in white-ruled South Africa, they needed to find common ground.

On January 8, 1912, three black lawyers called for an African congress modeled after the US Congress in Washington, DC. One hundred people attended the first meeting of the South African Native National Congress, later renamed the African National Congress (ANC). John Dube, a Zulu missionary and writer, was elected the first president. Members were the elite of South Africa's blacks—tribal chiefs and professionals educated in mission schools and overseas. They challenged the exclusion of blacks from politics and petitioned for basic civil rights. But they were facing overwhelming opposition from the white government. The fight would not be won easily.

The ANC was a political party and black nationalist organization. The leaders began to organize demonstrations and protests. But they were not radicals, and they did not advocate the use of violence. In those early years, the ANC made few inroads, and South Africa's blacks continued to struggle.

Support from Gandhi

The government paid little attention to the new black organization, but others took notice. A young lawyer from India named Mohandas K. Gandhi had been organizing the Indians in South Africa. Starting in the 1860s, Indian laborers and traders had settled in Natal, a city on the east coast. In 1906, Gandhi led peaceful protests against a proposed law to require all Asian males to be fingerprinted and carry an identity pass. When the law went into effect anyway, Gandhi was arrested for failing

Indian lawyer Mohandas K. Gandhi, wearing a Hindu cap, sits with his staff at his law office in Johannesburg in 1903. Before he led India's fight for independence from Great Britain, Gandhi battled for civil rights for Indians in South Africa.

to register. He served over seven months in prison for that and other protests during his time in Africa. Gandhi would later return to India to lead the nonviolent fight to free India from Great Britain.

At first, Gandhi did not think that Indians and blacks had shared interests. But with the new racist laws affecting both groups, he realized they needed each other's support. In his newspaper, *Indian Opinion*, Gandhi reprinted a letter written by Dube, the new ANC president. Gandhi called Dube "our friend and neighbor" and wrote the headline himself: "The Awakening of Africa."[7]

Mohandas K. Gandhi used the word *satyagraha* to describe the nonviolent protests he led against racist laws in South Africa. He said, "Truth (*satya*) implies love, and firmness (*agraha*) engenders and therefore serves as a synonym for force. I thus began to call the Indian movement 'satyagraha,' that is to say, the Force which is born of Truth and Love or non-violence."[8]

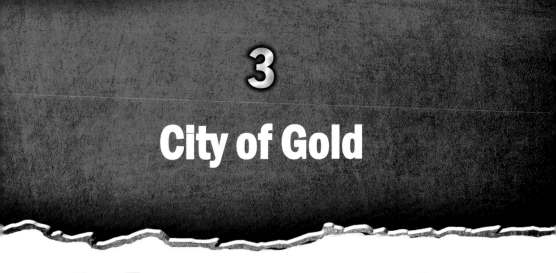

3
City of Gold

Mandela and his cousin Justice arrived in Johannesburg late one night in April 1941. They were amazed at the electricity lighting the streets, the colorful billboards, and the noisy traffic.

The grand steps of City Hall in Johannesburg in the 1940s were a far cry from the grassy paths of Qunu where Mandela grew up. The city was built on the wealth of gold mines and the labor of black workers.

Nicknamed the "City of Gold" for its large gold-mining industry, Johannesburg was a place where one could transform from "a poor peasant to a wealthy sophisticate," as Mandela would write later.[1] World War II had brought more people to the city, as well as more strain and food shortages. Still, Johannesburg seemed vibrant with possibilities.

Unfortunately, Mandela had almost no money and no job prospects. Blacks were not allowed to travel without permits and letters from an employer, which Mandela and his cousin did not have. He and Justice had left the regent without permission, a dangerous risk for Xhosas who were obligated to obey their tribal leaders. He needed to find employment quickly.

The next morning, the two went straight to the Crown Mines on a hill outside the city. The gold-mining company hired black workers for hazardous labor deep underground. Because of their education and royal roots, they managed to get better jobs—his cousin as a clerk, and Mandela as a night watchman.

Mandela's job was not difficult. He stood at the compound entrance and checked people's passes. But the job did not last. Mandela's boss discovered that the young men had defied the regent, and he planned to send them directly back to the Transkei. This would be a disaster for both of them.

Instead, the two went to see a friend of the regent's named Dr. Alfred B. Xuma, a respected physician who was president of the ANC. Unfortunately, Xuma's efforts to help them regain their jobs were not successful. Mandela was now in serious trouble. He had no job, home, or future—not to mention, he risked arrest for being in Johannesburg illegally.

Law Clerk

A cousin arranged for Mandela to meet an estate agent named Walter Sisulu. Perhaps Sisulu would have a job for him. A former cowherd, mine worker, and factory worker, Sisulu did not have a formal education, but he was interested in workers' rights and African history. He liked Mandela immediately, and the two would become lifelong friends. "When he came to my office, I marked him at once as a man with great qualities, who was destined to play an important part," Sisulu said of their first meeting.[2] Sisulu helped Mandela get a job as an articled clerk, or intern, in a white law office.

Working in the law office was an excellent opportunity, since Mandela was interested in becoming a lawyer one day. Along with earning a steady paycheck and learning about the law, Mandela met new people. An office mate took him to meetings and parties, where he met liberal white writers, black activists, and Communists. Communism is a political theory that supports a classless society where production is owned in common and there is no private property. The ideas of communism had taken hold in a small segment of South Africa's intellectuals. Mandela would never become a Communist, but the antiapartheid struggle would receive support from the Communists.

Meanwhile, Mandela was living in the black township of Alexandra, known as "Dark City" for its lack of electricity. Mandela's friend Xuma rented him a room in a tin-roofed shack without heat or plumbing. Hungry dogs barked day and night. Fortunately, a Methodist church was nearby, where Mandela worshipped.

Signs like this one were posted in Sophiatown in Johannesburg and District Six in Cape Town after the forced removal of black residents in the 1950s and 1960s.

Mandela earned barely enough money to survive. Sometimes, he walked the 12 miles (19 km) to work. Other times, he took a bus. Even so, he managed to finish his university work by correspondence to earn his BA degree from Fort Hare in early 1943. For the graduation ceremony, he borrowed money for a new suit from his friend Sisulu.

Bus Boycott

Determined to be a lawyer, Mandela enrolled in law studies at the University of the Witwatersrand in 1943. The Johannesburg university allowed a few black students, but they had to endure segregation. Blacks were not allowed to play sports on the fields or swim in the university pool. "When he sat at a table in the law library, a white student moved away," writes biographer Anthony Sampson.[3] It was no different off campus.

One day, Mandela and two Indian friends boarded a tram in Johannesburg. Indians were allowed to ride the tram, but blacks were not. The driver called Mandela a derogatory name and told his friends that he could not get on the tram. Mandela's friends protested, and a policeman arrested all three. Fortunately, the judge let them go. Later, Mandela would tell his former classmates, "I am what I am both as a result of people who respected me and helped me, and of those who did not respect me and treated me badly."[4] Fellow students saw Mandela as shy but dignified and the best-dressed student on campus.

His interest in politics grew stronger. In 1943, bus fares went up, causing serious problems for people in Alexandra. Activists began a boycott in which blacks refused to ride the buses. Mandela participated in the boycott, which lasted nine days and succeeded in lowering the fares. The power of a peaceful boycott made a lasting impression on Mandela. He saw that nonviolent protest could make a difference. Then, one night a friend took him to a meeting of the ANC. Mandela had found a home.

TOWNSHIPS

Starting in the nineteenth century, South Africa's blacks were forced to live apart from whites. Residential areas, known as townships, grew on the outskirts of large cities. The residents provided cheap labor for white homes and businesses. The townships grew during World War II as more people sought work in cities. Under apartheid, townships remained underdeveloped, often with substandard, crowded housing and no indoor plumbing or electricity. Transportation was inadequate, and schools had few supplies. Today, South Africa's townships continue to struggle with poverty and crowding, but some, like Soweto, also contain neighborhoods with new houses for the growing black middle class.

ANC Youth League

Three decades had passed since the founding of the ANC. Blacks in South Africa had made few inroads and still lacked fundamental rights. Mandela and other members were impatient with the slow progress. One night in the winter of 1944, they met with Xuma, the ANC president, at his fine house. They proposed a Youth League that would take more risky, aggressive action.

On Easter Sunday, April 9, 1944, Mandela joined his comrades at the Bantu Men's Social Center. The building was an important meeting place for blacks in Johannesburg. On this day, the ANC Youth League was formed. Mandela sat on the executive committee with his friends Sisulu and Oliver Tambo. The president of the ANC Youth League was a former teacher, Anton Lembede. Together, they would fight for a nonracial South Africa.

Mandela and the Youth League did not favor pushing white people out of Africa. They simply wanted to put an end to racism and white supremacy. They called the policy African nationalism. The ANC adopted the Youth League's policies and methods in 1949. Boycotts, strikes, civil disobedience, and noncooperation would be used to gain basic human and civil rights for the blacks of South Africa.

> **"The color of my skin is beautiful like the black soil of Mother Africa."—Anton Lembede, Zulu intellectual, teacher, and the first president of the ANC Youth League[5]**

Mandela was a snappy dresser and always wore a handkerchief in his pocket, as shown in this photo taken in January 1950, when he became president of the African National Congress Youth League.

Marriage and Family

Around this time, Mandela fell in love with a nursing student named Evelyn Ntoko Mase. She was Walter Sisulu's cousin and the daughter of a mine worker. Like Mandela, Mase had come to the city from the Transkei. The couple married in 1944 in a court in Johannesburg. They had no money for a traditional Xhosa ceremony.

They moved into a two-room house in Soweto, the sprawling Johannesburg township, where gold miners and day workers raised their families. The house at 8115 Orlando West would be Mandela's address from 1946 to 1962. (It is now the Nelson Mandela National Museum.) The house had a tin roof and a bucket for a toilet out back. "It was the opposite of grand, but it was my first true home of my own and I was mightily proud," he remembered later.[6] The next year, the couple had a son, Thembi. A daughter, Makaziwe, died in infancy.

Mandela had to make time for his books, his job as a law clerk, politics, and his growing family. He also liked to box at a local gym. Boxing was a sport where he could use his quick reflexes and combative personality. Throughout his life, he would struggle to balance his personal life with his devotion to law and politics. Mase would be the first of Mandela's three wives.

Crackdown

World War II ended in 1945. South Africa had fought on the side of the British. Only whites were allowed to serve in combat duty, but blacks, Indians, and coloureds drove ambulances and worked for the war effort on the home front. Jan Smuts, who was descended from Dutch settlers, served as South Africa's prime minister from 1939 to 1946. He believed in segregation between the races. After the war, Smuts began crackdowns on blacks and Indians, despite their wartime loyalty.

In August 1946, gold miners went on strike in Witwatersrand, one of the largest mines. The unionized black workers demanded better pay, food, and working conditions. The mining companies fought back. In the ensuing violence, nine miners were killed. The strike leaders were arrested, and several went to jail. The ANC was shocked by the government's harsh reaction.

Soon after, Smuts took action against the Indians in Natal. The new Ghetto Act of 1946 took away their rights to live and work in white areas and reduced their voice in government. Despite huge protests, the government prevailed.

The clouds were darkening. An important general election was coming in 1948. South Africa would have to decide the way forward. Would the country direct itself toward a more equal and democratic society? Or would the lines between the races be drawn deeper in the sand? The decision would not be up to Mandela and the ANC. As black South Africans, they were denied a vote for the future of their own country.

4

Freedom Fighter

A ll eyes were on the national election of 1948. The main issues were race and economics. Two parties were vying for power. Prime Minister Jan Smuts headed the United Party. He supported the

Attorney Nelson Mandela represented twenty-one women charged with disturbing the peace while protesting the Bantu Education Act that enforced segregation in schools.

country's racial policies, but he believed that gradual change was inevitable and that South Africa had to move toward integration. Because of the difficult war years, many voters were disenchanted with Smuts. They were looking for a change.

On the other side was the National Party, led by Afrikaner nationalists. Afrikaners were the descendants of the Boer farmers who colonized South Africa, as well as of German and French immigrants. Many were farmers who resented the wealthier British. Some Afrikaners supported Nazi Germany during the war, rather than South Africa's ally, Great Britain. Afrikaners were eager to take charge and defend their culture.

The National Party favored white supremacy, racial segregation, and laws to control the black workers on whom the Boers relied for labor. The National Party leader, Dr. Daniel Malan, ran his campaign on a platform of apartheid. "Apartheid" is an Afrikaans word meaning "apartness," and Malan promised voters a hardening of the racial laws. As Mandela recounted in his autobiography, the nationalists had a motto that meant in English, "The white man must always remain boss."[1]

While the ballots were counted on May 26, Mandela was attending an all-night ANC meeting. Just because they couldn't vote did not mean they weren't anxious for results. When Mandela and his friends saw the morning headlines, they were shocked. The National Party had won a narrow victory. Apartheid was now the rule of the land. The racist oppression they had fought so hard to end could become even worse.

Apartheid

Their fears were soon realized. In the next years, the government passed a series apartheid laws that stripped blacks, Indians, and coloureds of political, economic, and human rights. The government also took away their legal rights and gave them little opportunity to defend themselves. Arrest, detention, and incarceration became tools to suppress the majority population. Police did not need warrants to search homes.

Apartheid had specific purposes. One was to give South African whites both political and economic power. Another purpose of apartheid was to unite the British and Afrikaners against a common foe. To enforce apartheid, the list of new laws grew every year. The vote was taken away from coloureds. Blacks were moved to tribal homelands. Marriage between whites and other races was prohibited.

One of the key laws that made apartheid enforceable was the Population Registration Act of 1950. The law required that South African be classified by race based on physical features such as the color of skin or texture of hair. People were identified at birth and registered as belonging to one of four racial groups: white, coloured, Bantu (black), and other. Later, Asian was added as a category. People had to carry their identity document at all times. Families were torn apart if their relatives or spouses had different skin colors, because they couldn't live in the same areas. This racial law helped the government enforce other laws.

Segregation between the races was also made stricter. Signs that said "Europeans Only" or "Non-Europeans Only" were posted on public buildings, rail station waiting rooms, and restrooms. A 1953 law, the Bantu Education Act, enforced segregation in schools and universities. The laws on segregation even stated that separate facilities need not be equal. Another law, the Group Areas Act, restricted people by race from living in certain areas. Using this law, police and army troops in 1955 forced thousands to abandon their homes in Sophiatown. A hub of jazz, black culture, and the ANC, Sophiatown had expanded too close to a white neighborhood. Houses were razed, and a white suburb rose on the land.

The government used force to suppress the black resistance. Police and security officials broke up meetings and rounded up dissidents. South Africa tried to undermine the leaders of the ANC and other organizations by imprisoning, banning, and forcing them into exile. Within a decade, the white minority held almost complete power over the blacks, who made up the majority of the population. South Africa had become one of the most racist nations in the world. The question was what Mandela and the ANC could possibly do to change its course.

Defiance Campaign

The ANC had to fight back. The older leaders were reluctant to provoke the government, but Mandela and the younger activists were not. On June 26, 1950,

A black woman defies the "Europeans Only" sign on the rail car on September 2, 1952, during the apartheid regime of Daniel Malan in South Africa.

they launched the Day of Protest, a national political strike. There were demonstrations in the streets, and blacks stayed home from work and did not open their businesses. Today, Freedom Day is celebrated in South Africa every June 26 to honor the first national strike against apartheid.

More needed to be done. In 1951, the ANC decided on a campaign of passive resistance to pressure the government to repeal apartheid laws. The ANC activists could not do it alone. Even though the ANC had not always seen eye-to-eye with Indian and coloured groups, they needed each other's support.

> "I, the undersigned, Volunteer of the National Volunteer Corps, do hereby solemnly pledge and bind myself to serve my country and my people in accordance with the directives of the National Volunteer Corps and to participate fully and without reservations to the best of my ability in the Campaign for the Defiance of Unjust Laws."—Defiance Campaign pledge[2]

Coming together, the ANC, the South African Indian Congress, and the Coloured People's Congress launched the Defiance Campaign. Mandela was named volunteer in chief of the biggest nonviolent resistance campaign in South Africa. The intent was to break apartheid laws requiring blacks to carry passes, obey curfews, and keep out of white areas. Trained volunteers would act together in groups.

On June 26, 1952, fifty-two Indian and black volunteers marched into a neighborhood near Johannesburg

BANNED!

In 1952, Mandela was "banned" by the South African government for two years. He couldn't attend public meetings or gatherings, even his son's birthday party. Bans against Mandela continued on and off for the next decade. He wasn't alone. Some sixteen hundred people were banned during apartheid from 1948 to 1991. They could not leave their local area and had to report to the police once a week. They could not go to the airport, travel to see relatives, or publish newspapers. Some were placed under house arrest, meaning that they had to stay at home, except to go to work. Banning was one more way the apartheid government tried to repress the opposition and subjugate the people.

without their proper permits. They held their hands in a fist to show strength in unity, with their thumbs up to represent optimism that their struggle would succeed, and they sang the freedom anthem "Nkosi Sikilel' iAfrika," meaning "God Bless, Africa!"[3] Similar actions took place around the city.

The government responded quickly. That night, Mandela was with a small group of protestors that left a hall after curfew; they were all arrested. Another group walked into a white entrance at the railway station. They, too, were arrested. In the next six months, the campaign spread to other cities and towns. By December, over eight thousand people had been arrested.[4]

Lawyer

Meanwhile, Mandela had to earn a living. In 1952, he and his friend Oliver Tambo hung up a brass sign with their names at the Chancellor House, a small building across from the Magistrate's Court in Johannesburg. Theirs was the first black-owned law firm in South Africa. The lawyers provided affordable counsel, and clients lined up outside the door. Many had done nothing more than break an apartheid law. "It was a crime to walk through a Whites Only door, a crime to ride a Whites Only bus, a crime to use a Whites Only drinking fountain," Mandela recalled.[5]

He became known as a dedicated lawyer who fought hard for his clients. It wasn't easy being a black lawyer in apartheid South Africa. Often, Mandela was challenged in court because of his race. Witnesses refused to answer his questions. The judge questioned his right to practice law. The law firm was threatened with eviction from the building.

But Mandela always held his head high. In court, he was dramatic and assertive, using

South African activist and lawyer Oliver Tambo (*left*) meets with his close friend Mandela in Johannesburg, on December 6, 1990. The two men owned the first black law firm in South Africa.

his arms to gesture. "I did not act as though I were a black man in a white man's court," he wrote.[6] He knew how important he was to his clients. "I realized quickly what Mandela and Tambo meant to ordinary Africans. It was a place where ... they would not be either turned away or cheated, a place where they might actually feel proud to be represented by men of their own skin color," he noted.[7]

Arrest

On July 30, 1952, Mandela was working late at the office when police burst in the door. They arrested him for a violation of the Suppression of Communism Act, not because he was a member of the Communist Party, but because he had opposed the government in the Defiance Campaign. In September, Mandela was put on trial in Johannesburg with twenty-one other ANC and Indian activists. On December 2, they were all found guilty. The judge sentenced them to nine months imprisonment with hard labor, but he suspended the sentence for two years because the campaign had been nonviolent.

Despite the arrests and lack of progress, the Defiance Campaign was deemed successful. "The campaign freed me from any lingering sense of doubt or inferiority I might still have felt; it liberated me from the feeling of being overwhelmed by the power and seeming invincibility of the white man and his institutions. I had come of age as a freedom fighter," Mandela wrote.[8] Meanwhile, the world was taking notice. The UN established a commission to investigate South Africa. But, for Mandela, life was even more stressful. In the fall of 1952, he and other ANC leaders had been banned by the government. The banning order meant, among other restrictions, that he could not go to meetings or speak out in public. For now, he would have to continue the struggle against apartheid out of sight of the government.

Freedom Charter

The Defiance Campaign had not changed the status quo. New efforts were needed. In 1955, the Congress of the People campaign took off. The campaign was aimed at establishing a "freedom charter," listing the demands of the people of South Africa. Many organizations came together in this unifying campaign, including trade unions. Because the campaign offered such a broad appeal, people from all parts of South African society who were affected by apartheid offered suggestions for the charter. On June 25 and 26, 1955, the groups gathered at a huge conference in Kliptown, outside Johannesburg. The Congress of the People drafted a freedom charter for a nonracial, democratic, and united South Africa. Never before had so many people come together in the cause of freedom. Perhaps now the South African government would start to listen.

5

Spear of the Nation

On December 5, 1956, Mandela woke up to loud knocks on his door. Carrying warrants, three white policemen searched his house and arrested him for high treason and conspiracy to overthrow the government. Some 155 antiapartheid leaders were arrested that night.

Mandela speaks with some of his co-defendants outside the Treason Trial in the late 1950s in Johannesburg, South Africa.

Those arrested were taken to the Fort, the city prison on a hill above Johannesburg. Under apartheid, blacks had few legal protections. The right to habeas corpus, or to challenge the reasons for a person's arrest and detention, was suspended, and the government allowed indefinite detention. Two weeks later, the men were taken to an old military building used for a courtroom. They were put in a wire cage until their lawyers successfully demanded that the cage be removed. The prosecutor read a lengthy indictment. To win the case against them, the government would have to prove that they had used violence.

The prisoners were allowed to go home while the case went forward. At first, Mandela was optimistic that the charges against him would be dropped. He thought the Treason Trial, as it became known, was only a means for the government to silence the antiapartheid leaders. He did not know that the long trial, which would last from 1956 to 1961, would cause him years of uncertainty.

During the Treason Trial, Mandela separated from his wife, Evelyn. He met a spirited woman named Nomzamo Winifred Madikizela, also from the Transkei. Sixteen years younger than Mandela, Winnie was the first black social worker in a large hospital in Johannesburg. In June 1958, they were married. Winnie became Mandela's partner in the antiapartheid struggle. They had two daughters, Zenani and Zindziswa. But they would live many years apart when Mandela was imprisoned. In the end, the marriage would not last.

Sharpeville Massacre

Outrage over apartheid grew to a furor by 1960. That year, both the ANC and the Pan-Africanist Congress, another

A peaceful protest against the pass laws turns into a national tragedy after police fire on protestors on March 21, 1960, in the township of Sharpeville.

antiapartheid group, decided to protest the racist pass laws. Of all apartheid laws, the pass laws, requiring blacks to carry identification at all times, were most detested. Too many people had been arrested simply for not carrying their pass books. The protests were expected to be large but nonviolent.

On March 21, 1960, about five thousand unarmed anti-pass protestors gathered around the police station in Sharpeville, a black township south of Johannesburg. Police did not wait to be provoked before firing into the crowds. At least sixty-nine blacks were killed, and more than two hundred were wounded. The police later said that they were defending themselves against rocks, but only a few police were hit by rocks. On March 30, Mandela was arrested in his house. No reason was given by police.

The Sharpeville Massacre was a crisis for the apartheid government. It ignited a firestorm of disapproval from the international community. South Africa's stock market fell. The government clamped down even harder. A state of emergency was called, allowing arrests without specific charges, and all political meetings were banned. The government also banned the ANC and the Pan-Africanist Congress.

Mandela was released from jail quickly because the Treason Trial had finally come to an end. He was expected in court to hear the verdict on March 30, 1961. The news was good. The judge stated that it was "impossible for this court to come to the conclusion that the African National Congress has acquired or adopted a policy to overthrow the state by violence."[1] Mandela and his codefendants were found innocent. But the government was not happy with the verdict and would continue to harass Mandela until he was back behind bars.

PASS BOOKS

Even before apartheid began in 1948, South African blacks over age sixteen had to carry "native passes." Not doing so meant arrest and a trial, and possibly a fine or jail. During apartheid, the pass books held a person's photograph, address, marital status, education, employment, and eventually, race, along with other information. The books could be pages long. Blacks were not allowed in a white area without special permission, such as a work contract. That information had to be in the pass books, as well. Thousands were arrested during apartheid for not producing a pass book when stopped by police.

Underground

Meanwhile, Mandela, under banning orders, had to live mostly underground. Unable to gather with others in groups or speak in public, he could only meet with his ANC comrades in secret. Traveling around the country to gain support for the ANC, Mandela took to wearing disguises and going out only after dark. He disguised himself as a chauffeur, a chef, or sometimes a gardener. He wore the blue overalls of a worker and round, rimless glasses. Sometimes, he wore a chauffeur's cap when he was driving, on the pretense that he was driving his "master's car."[2]

Even underground, Mandela was helping the ANC make plans. The next event was a nationwide strike in which workers would simply stay at home. The strike was scheduled for May 29. On that day, thousands of people walked out of factories or did not leave their homes to go to work. But the strike was not as successful as the ANC had hoped, and it was called off quickly.

Despite the obstacles, Mandela was determined to keep fighting. On June 26, 1961, Freedom Day, Mandela wrote a statement to the press in which he explained why he chose to go underground rather than leave the country. He vowed to continue the struggle against apartheid. "For my own part I have made my choice. I will not leave South Africa, nor will I surrender. Only through hardship, sacrifice and militant action can freedom be won. The struggle is my life. I will continue fighting for freedom until the end of my days," he wrote.[3]

Spear of the Nation

Nonviolent strikes and protests had failed to end apartheid. Perhaps Mandela and his comrades had to put aside the ANC philosophy of peaceful change. He began to think that violence might be a necessary tactic to dismantle apartheid. He used an African expression to describe his new position: "The attacks of the wild beast cannot be averted with only bare hands," Mandela said.[4]

In December 1961, he cofounded the militant wing of the ANC. It was called Umkhonto we Sizwe, or Spear of the Nation, and commonly referred to as the MK. (The spear is a traditional African weapon.) The intention of the MK was not to kill people, but rather to undermine the government. The activists would target buildings, power stations, and other government locations connected with apartheid. The MK declared that it would "hit back by all means within our power in defense of our people, our future and our freedom."[5]

The night of December 16, 1961, five bombs went off in Port Elizabeth in the Eastern Cape. The homemade devices set by the MK hit an electric power station and other government buildings. More attacks followed. In the next eighteen months, more than two hundred locations were bombed in the Eastern Cape. Bombs also went off in Pretoria and Johannesburg. The locations hit were pass offices and other facilities that supported the apartheid system.

During this time, Mandela and other MK members hid out at the Liliesleaf Farm in Rivonia in suburban Johannesburg. The quiet farm was a place of refuge. Out of earshot of the government, they planned attacks and plotted the future. One of the problems they faced was that the MK needed better support and military training. For that, they needed to go outside of South Africa.

Guerrilla Training

Mandela was sent to Ethiopia in February 1962 to attend a conference for the African freedom movement. He had to sneak out of South Africa secretly, and illegally. In Ethiopia, he met dignitaries and gave a speech at the conference. Later, he traveled to Egypt, Tunisia, Morocco, and other African countries. He raised money for weapons and gathered support for his cause. Mandela went on to London, where he met with antiapartheid activists and journalists. This was his first experience on the world stage—but not his last.

He returned to Ethiopia, where he spent two months training for MK raids and sabotage. Guerrilla fighters taught him how to hold and fire a gun. He didn't get much chance to put his new skills to practice. Mandela returned to South Africa and, while driving a car wearing a chauffer's outfit, was arrested again on August 5, 1962. His life as a rebel in hiding was over. For the next twenty-seven years, Mandela would either be on trial or imprisoned.

> "It is said that no one truly knows a nation until one has been inside its jails. A nation should not be judged by how it treats its highest citizens, but its lowest ones—and South Africa treated its imprisoned African citizens like animals."[6]

White Man's Court

The trial began in the fall of 1962. Mandela was charged with leaving the country illegally and inciting a strike. On October 15, Mandela wore a traditional Xhosa garment, called the *kaross*, when he walked into the old synagogue that served as a court in Pretoria. "I had chosen traditional dress to emphasize the symbolism that I was a black African walking into a white man's court," he wrote in his autobiography.[7] His wife, Winnie, was in the courtroom dressed in her own traditional Xhosa clothing.

The kaross, Mandela wrote, was also a sign of contempt for the white justice system. His supporters cheered with their fists clenched. On his way back to his cell, the officials tried to take his kaross, but Mandela refused to give it up. In a compromise, they agreed he could wear it in court but not elsewhere, for fear it would incite other prisoners.

A week later, Mandela was allowed to speak to the court. He said that the trial was unfair because he was a "black man in a white man's court" and was not being tried by "his own flesh and blood."[8] The trial went on. More than one hundred witnesses were called by the prosecution to testify that Mandela had left the country illegally and that he had encouraged African workers to strike in May 1961. Knowing he was guilty, Mandela wasn't surprised when he received a five-year prison sentence for leaving the country without a passport. He began serving the sentence in the Pretoria jail. A year later, Mandela faced new charges for the more serious crime of sabotage. Along with his closest ANC comrades, this time Mandela would go on trial for his life.

6
Prisoner #466/64

On July 11, 1963, fourteen police officers raided the Liliesleaf Farm in Rivonia, where ANC and MK leaders were hiding out. The police searched the house; found incriminating letters, maps, and other documents relating to sabotage activities; and arrested eight suspects, including Mandela's friend Walter Sisulu. Mandela was not there, because he was already in prison. His name was added to the list of defendants.

The charges were announced on October 9 in the Hall of Justice in Pretoria: two counts of conspiracy and two counts of sabotage. The charges were serious, particularly with a new apartheid law against sabotage. The defendants, if found guilty, could receive the death penalty. As they listened to the charges, they were not allowed to wear street clothes but instead wore the prison uniform of khaki shorts and shirts. Mandela later wrote that he felt humiliated in those clothes.

Mandela and the other defendants decided that they would use the court proceedings as an opportunity to argue their case against apartheid and to build pressure against the government. Their argument was that South Africa's laws were established without people's consent. A new system had to be created based on a nonracial constitution that respected human rights.

Winnie Mandela leaves the Palace of Justice in Pretoria on June 16, 1964, after the verdict of the Rivonia Trial. Her husband, Nelson Mandela, and his comrades had just been sentenced to life imprisonment for their anti-apartheid activities.

As the trial got underway at the end of October, the courtroom was full every day. The newspapers were full of stories about the dangerous revolutionaries on trial. In the streets, supporters gathered with signs and hope that the ANC leaders would be able to survive the trial. All of South Africa—and the world at large—was anxious to see what would happen.

Prepared to Die

For months, the prosecution aired its case, accusing Mandela and the others of 222 acts of sabotage. The prosecution detailed how the ANC built bombs and gathered money from other countries, and implied the ANC supported the Communists. At last it was time for the defense. Mandela chose to give a statement instead of being interrogated. On April 20, 1964, he stood up in the dock in front of the courtroom and read from a handwritten document. The speech would later be called "I Am Prepared to Die." In the speech, Mandela admitted that he had organized sabotage, but he also explained his reasons: "I do not, however, deny that I planned sabotage. I did not plan it in a spirit of recklessness nor because I have any love of violence. I planned it as a result of a calm and sober assessment of the political situation that had arisen after many years of tyranny, exploitation, and oppression of my people by whites."[1]

He also spoke about his dreams of a South Africa where blacks could own land, live where they chose, be paid a living wage, and do worthwhile work. "Above all, we want equal political rights, because without them our disabilities will be permanent. I know this sounds revolutionary to the whites in this country, because the majority of voters will be Africans. This makes the white man fear democracy," he said.[2] In the end, he said, a democratic and free society in which "all persons live together in harmony and with equal opportunities" was an idea for which he was "prepared to die."[3]

Despite his stirring speech, the government prevailed. Mandela and seven others—Walter Sisulu, Govan Mbeki, Raymond Mhlaba, Elias Motsoaledi, Ahmed Kathrada, and Denis Goldberg—were convicted of conspiracy and sabotage. Two other defendants were acquitted. On Friday, June 12, 1964, the prisoners received their sentences. The judge did not impose the death penalty. Instead, he sentenced them to life in prison.

Outside in the streets, people responded to the verdict by shouting, "Amandla! Ngawethu!" They held up the clenched fist and upright thumb in solidarity with the ANC. The African anthem filled the air.[4] In the prison van outside the court, the prisoners held up clenched fists in the windows. They were not giving up the fight. Yet hope was dimming. Mandela was forty-six-years-old. He could spend the rest of his life behind bars.

"I and some colleagues came to the conclusion that as violence in this country was inevitable, it would be wrong and unrealistic for African leaders to continue preaching peace and non-violence at a time when the government met our peaceful demands with force. It was only when all else had failed, when all channels of peaceful protest had been barred to us, that the decision was made to embark on violent forms of political struggle."[5]

Prison

Mandela and the others—except for the one white prisoner, who was sent to a white prison—were flown to an island in Table Bay 6 miles (9.7 km) off the coast of Cape Town. Robben Island looked green and lush from a distance, but white sharks swam in the waters, and Mandela, who had been imprisoned there two years earlier, knew the rough conditions he could expect in the prison. Robben Island was where Xhosa warriors had been banished by the British in the nineteenth century. The island had later been a leper colony and a naval base. Now, it was the site of one of the most notorious maximum-security prisons in South Africa.

Mandela and his comrades were taken to the stone cell block for political prisoners. It was one story, with a courtyard in the center and cells on three sides. The last side was a high wall patrolled by guards and dogs.[6] Each prisoner had his or her own cell, with one small window with iron bars. Prisoners had to sleep on a straw mat with thin blankets on the stone floor. Outside his cell, Mandela's prisoner number was posted: "N. Mandela 466/64."

The prisoners had little time to rest. Stones were dumped in a pile at the entrance to the courtyard, and the prisoners spent their days using hammers to crush the stones into gravel. The work was both boring and tiring, and the prisoners were often cold in the winter weather.

The prison was as racially divided as South Africa. The guards were Afrikaners, and the prisoners were black. Still, Mandela craved respect. One of his first gestures was to ask for long pants, rather than the prison shorts. He was given pants, but he refused to wear them unless the other prisoners also wore pants. "We would fight inside

As South Africa's president in 1995, Mandela shows journalists how he spent his days chipping limestone rocks under the hot sun during his long imprisonment on Robben Island.

as we had fought outside. The racism and repression were the same. I would simply have to fight on different terms," he wrote later.[7] He would not despair.

The World Is Watching

For decades, the world had stood by as black South Africans suffered under apartheid. But the Rivonia Trial drew attention to the racist system—and international outrage began to grow. The 1960s were the height of the civil rights movement in the United States, and the cry for equality echoed across the ocean. People on all around the globe were impatient for racial segregation to end.

ANTI-APARTHEID MOVEMENT

Boycotts against South African products began in Great Britain in 1959. Student unions banned South African fruit and cigarettes from campuses, and shoppers were asked not to buy products made by companies that supported apartheid. The Sharpeville shootings in 1960 spurred the creation of the Anti-Apartheid Movement (AAM). The AAM pushed banks to divest in South Africa and raised money to support the ANC. Until 1994, when Nelson Mandela became president of a free, nonracial South Africa, the AAM kept the issue in the news, gathering more supporters every year.

On August 18, 1964, the International Olympic Committee barred South Africa from competing in the Summer Olympics in Tokyo that fall. The decision was made after South Africa refused to condemn apartheid. The committee stated that the only way the country could rejoin Olympic competition would be to end segregation in sports and to renounce racial discrimination. Other sporting organizations and individual athletes joined the protest against South Africa's apartheid.

It wasn't only the sports world that took a stand. In 1963, the UN called for an international arms embargo to South Africa. The embargo was made mandatory in 1977. The UN also asked world nations to stop supplying oil to South Africa. In 1968, a cultural embargo was declared by the UN, urging nations to "suspend cultural, educational, sporting and other exchanges with the racist regime."[8] The United States stopped selling arms to South Africa but did not go any further.

Like many other countries, the United States continued to treat South Africa as an ally and business partner, and trade went on as usual. Great Britain's close ties with South Africa ensured continued support, despite a growing antiapartheid movement. Other major trading partners of South Africa were also reluctant to take a stand against apartheid.

Robben Island

In 1965, Mandela began working in the limestone quarry on Robben Island. The work was backbreaking, and the dust and harsh sunlight damaged his vision. The prisoners protested the hard labor, and by 1977 they won the argument: manual labor like working in the quarry was no longer required of prisoners. Other rules remained that made life difficult. For the slightest infraction, such as not standing when the warden came into the room, prisoners were punished with isolation. Once, Mandela was caught reading a newspaper someone left on a bench, although this was against prison regulations. In isolation, Mandela received rice water three times a day and no food.

Visits were rare. During his first years in prison, he lost both his mother and his eldest son, Madiba Thembekile (Thembi), who was killed in a car accident. Nor was he allowed to see his other children. His wife, Winnie, had been banned. She had to get special permission to see Mandela. Even then, visits were only thirty minutes long, and they had to speak through a window with guards listening close by.

Still, he kept up his spirits. Singing was not allowed, but when Mandela and his prison mates were sent to the limestone quarry, they sang anyway. "They wanted to break our spirits. So what we did was to sing freedom songs as we were working and everybody was inspired," he later said.[9] Mandela's years inside prison were hardly wasted. He stayed up late at night to finish his law degree. He also used the time to deepen his ideas on how to end racism in South Africa. As a young man, Mandela was often impulsive and angry. In prison, he became calmer. He realized that negotiation and compromise, values of his Xhosa ancestors, might be necessary for change to occur.

Autobiography

In 1974, in his fifties, Mandela began writing his auto-biography. He was involved in many of the key historic events of his time, and he also was an active participant in trying to evoke change. His experiences reflected those of many South Africans in the twentieth century. Mandela had a lot to say. Every night, he'd write in secret. His fellow prisoners, including Walter Sisulu, helped him with the project. At one point, Mandela buried the manu-script in cocoa containers in the prison yard, but the cans were discovered. He was punished for four years with the loss of study privileges.[10] One friend rewrote the pages in shorthand. Still another prisoner smuggled the manu-script out of the prison.

The manuscript was smuggled to London, where ANC leader in exile Oliver Tambo was able to pass it on. Eventually, the book that described Mandela's childhood, the history of the ANC, and the antiapartheid struggle was delivered to print. *Long Walk to Freedom* was an interna-tional best seller when it was published by Little, Brown & Company in 1995. Mandela's life story was also made into a Hollywood film, *Mandela: Long Walk to Freedom*, in 2013.

7

Uprising

arly in the morning of June 16, 1976, ten thousand young people took to the streets of Soweto, the black township outside Johannesburg, to protest a new law that required them to study half their subjects in the Afrikaans language. Afrikaans was considered the language of oppression by many students. They wanted to be taught in English and their native tribal languages.

The police quickly gathered around the marchers. Rocks were thrown, and the police opened fire with tear gas and live ammunition. The protest turned violent. One of the people who died that day was a twelve-year-old boy named Hector Pieterson. A local journalist, Sam Nzima, took a photo of a teenager, Mbuyisa Makhubo, who had picked up the bleeding boy to carry him to a clinic, and a crying girl who accompanied them. The photo shocked the world.

The police reported 23 deaths in the Soweto Uprising, but later estimates were closer to 575. The tragedy was a turning point. The uprising and the deaths that resulted sparked new protests against police brutality and the racist government. From then on, students became more vocal, trade unions joined in, and protests against apart-

Mandela is shown in this 1960s-era photo sewing one of his prison uniforms, which he despised having to wear.

heid spread across South Africa. Meanwhile, the UN denounced the South African government for "its resort to massive violence against and killings of the African people including schoolchildren and students and others opposing racial discrimination."[1] June 16 has become Youth Day in South Africa to honor the children who died in the Soweto Uprising.

Illness

In March 1982, Mandela and other ANC prisoners, including Walter Sisulu, were transferred from Robben Island to Pollsmoor Prison, a less secure facility, outside Cape Town. He was given a new prison number, 220/82. The conditions in the new prison were slightly better. Mandela was allowed more comfortable visits with Winnie without a window separating them. It had been twenty-one years since they had touched hands. Even foreign dignitaries were allowed to visit Mandela, whose fame had grown.

Under growing public pressure, American companies began pulling out of South Africa in the 1980s. The US government was more reluctant. Fearing the loss of trade, the Reagan administration had supported the apartheid government and even put Mandela on the US terrorist watch list. In 1985, President Ronald Reagan vetoed a congressional proposal to impose economic sanctions on South Africa, but his veto was overturned. In 1986, after a long delay, the United States, Japan, and the European Community imposed economic sanctions on South Africa. More action followed. The US Congress passed legislation banning all new investments and bank loans in

South Africa; banned South African imports; and ended air travel between the United States and South Africa.

"Can we abandon a country that has stood by us in every war we've fought, a country that is strategically essential to the free world?"[2]—US president Ronald Reagan

South Africa risked economic collapse if apartheid continued. Members of the government began to reach out to Mandela. They knew that he was a key person in any possible negotiations. Mandela was taken from prison and driven to the house of the justice minister. The two men talked. For the antiapartheid movement, daylight was starting to break.

Mandela was not going to be won over easily. In 1988, P. W. Botha, now the president of South Africa, offered to release him from prison if he renounced violence. Mandela refused. He knew that this would show weakness and also turn the ANC against him. Soon after, he underwent surgery for prostate cancer. After he recovered, he continued talking with the government. Finding common ground would take time.

In 1988, Mandela became ill with tuberculosis, a serious disease of the lungs. After he was well, in December 1988, he was moved to Victor Verster Prison in today's Western Cape Province. It was a farm prison for prisoners who were getting ready to be released. No longer was he to be confined in a prison cell. He moved into a former prison guard's cottage and had a swimming pool, a garden, and a personal cook. It was apparent that the government wanted its most famous prisoner to be comfortable.

Free Mandela

Even while the government made gestures toward Mandela, crackdowns in the streets kept life difficult for black South Africans. In 1985, a state of emergency had been declared. The security forces detained prisoners without a trial, banned political meetings, and even stopped the media from publishing stories.

The cry "Free Nelson Mandela" grew louder. Musicians supported him with songs about freedom. Massive crowds packed Wembley Stadium in London on June 11, 1988, for the Nelson Mandela 70th Birthday Tribute. The concert was meant to bring attention to Mandela and his cause. It hadn't been easy to organize. Some musicians were reluctant to participate. The organizers received bomb threats, and conservative members of the British Parliament questioned whether the concert was supporting the so-called terrorist activities of the ANC.

The concert went on anyway. Big-name artists like Sting, Harry Belafonte, Whitney Houston, and Stevie Wonder thrilled the crowds. Broadcast around the world, the event was a huge success. Songs performed that day included "Biko," sung by Peter Gabriel; "Amazing Grace," sung by Jessye Norman; and "Free Nelson Mandela," sung by Jerry Dammers.

Dismantling Apartheid

Under international and internal pressures, by the late 1980s, South Africa began to dismantle some apartheid laws, including the law prohibiting interracial marriage and the pass laws. More jobs opened to blacks, and black trade unions were recognized. Public facilities such as libraries, buses, parks, and restaurants were no longer segregated. But much of apartheid remained in place. People were still classified by race. Schools were segregated and unequal, and blacks were unable to own land. More change was needed before South Africa was a country for all people.

In December 1989, F. W. de Klerk, the new president of South Africa, visited Mandela. Born in 1939 in Johannesburg, de Klerk grew up in politics. His father was a member of the first apartheid government. De Klerk was conservative and had supported apartheid. Now de Klerk saw that apartheid threatened to ruin the country.

STEVE BIKO

Mandela was one of many who sacrificed their lives to fight apartheid. One of the fighters was a young man named Steve Biko. He was a student leader and a founder of the South African Students' Organisation, a group that advocated self-reliance and liberation for young blacks. He later started the Black Consciousness Movement to raise pride in African culture. He was often harassed and detained by the police. After being detained for distributing political pamphlets, he was questioned for hours, beaten, and left without medical care. On September 12, 1977, Biko died in a prison cell in Pretoria at age thirty. The cause of death was brain damage. His death sparked intense outrage and gave fresh urgency to the struggle to end apartheid.

Elected president only months earlier, de Klerk favored Mandela's release. Later, he would remember his first impressions. "He was taller than I expected—he was ramrod straight. He looked one in the eye very directly, he was a good listener and I could see very easily that he had an analytical approach to discussions, which I liked very much. I was really very impressed with him at that first meeting," de Klerk recalled.[3] Mandela felt that he could work with de Klerk. They had a shared interest in bringing peace to South Africa. "We both reached the conclusion that we would be able to do business with one another," said de Klerk.[4]

That same year, 1989, Mandela received a law degree from the University of South Africa. But he wasn't about to practice law again anytime soon. For now, South Africa remained a repressive, segregated society—and Mandela was still a political prisoner with a life sentence.

8

Freedom and Democracy

February 11, 1990, was a typical late summer day in South Africa. The weather was warm, without a cloud in the sky. In his cottage at Victor Verster

A triumphant Mandela, accompanied by his wife Winnie, walks out of Victor Verster prison on February 11, 1990, as a free man. His hand is raised in the ANC salute before a cheering crowd.

Prison, Mandela woke up at 4:30 a.m. and began preparing for his freedom. People came to give him their best wishes as he packed piles of books and papers collected over two decades. Mandela said good-bye to his longtime prison guard, James Gregory. Then his wife, Winnie, Walter Sisulu, and other ANC friends arrived to accompany him on his walk to freedom.

Shortly before 4:00 p.m., he and Winnie were driven to the front gate of the prison. A crowd of thousands, along with reporters and television cameras, was waiting to greet him. As he walked through the gate, Mandela raised his right fist in the ANC power salute, and the people erupted in a loud roar. "I had not been able to do that for twenty-seven years and it gave me a surge of strength and joy," he wrote later.[1] Even though he was seventy-one-years-old, Mandela felt his life was about to start again.

The government had lifted the ban on the ANC, but Mandela's comrades were not the only ones who welcomed him to freedom. Along the road to Cape Town, white families waved with their fists clenched as his car passed by. Perhaps South Africa had changed even more than he had expected.

A rally was planned in the center of Cape Town. Too many people filled the streets for Mandela's car to get through. Not surprisingly, he got nervous that the excitement at his release could spiral out of control. At last, as dusk fell, Mandela stood on the balcony of City Hall before a raucous crowd. People were shouting, crying, laughing, and singing. They waved banners and flags.

His speech that day was full of gratitude. "I stand before you not as a prophet but as a humble servant of you, the people. Your tireless and heroic sacrifices have made it possible for me to be here today," he said.[2]

Thousands of people flock to an African National Congress rally at Orlando Stadium in Soweto on February 12, 1990, to celebrate Mandela's release from prison and to hear him speak.

He paid respect to F. W. de Klerk, who had helped make this moment possible. Mandela also looked at the challenges that lay ahead. Already, as South African officials heard Mandela speak on his first day of freedom, some wondered why he was not distancing himself from the radical elements of the ANC. But Mandela knew that an unquestionable loyalty to the ANC was vital if the blacks of South Africa were to trust him. They needed to know he was on their side.

Negotiations

Formal negotiations to end apartheid between the National Party government and the ANC got underway. Mandela's ability as a leader was apparent, not just as a spokesperson for black South Africans, but as a force for compromise. People were amazed that Mandela expressed little anger about his long imprisonment. Instead, he chose to approach the future with a fresh gaze.

In truth, he was bitter, but he had learned to hide it. He once told his friend, former US president Bill Clinton, that he did have hard feelings

ings about his enemies when he walked out of prison for the last time. "I am old enough to tell the truth ... I felt hatred and fear but I said to myself, if you have them when you get in that car you will still be their prisoner. I wanted to be free and so I let go."[3] American writer Richard Stengel, who worked with Mandela on his autobiography, observed, "The man who went into prison in 1962 was hotheaded and easily stung. The man who walked out into the sunshine of the mall in Cape Town 27 years later was measured, even serene. It was a hard-won moderation. In prison, he learned to control his anger. He had no choice."[4]

In fact, Mandela held on to the steely determination that had always driven him. He may have forgiven his enemies, but he wouldn't be swayed from his goals. De Klerk and Mandela agreed that the ultimate goal was free democratic elections open to all South Africans and a new nonracial constitution.

Turmoil

The same year he was freed from prison, Mandela led an ANC meeting at which the organization renounced

Both lawyers, though from starkly different backgrounds, anti-apartheid leader Mandela (*right*) and South African President F.W. de Klerk (*left*) speak at a press conference in South Africa on May 4, 1990.

South African government still had its police and security forces, and the people had few defenses. But Mandela knew it was the only way forward. As one writer later noted, "Mandela chose peace over war; reconciliation over vengeance; humanity over barbarity."[5]

Meanwhile, the country, in a state of flux, fell into turmoil. Many of the apartheid-era laws had been dismantled but not all, and blacks were impatient for change. Unfortunately, during this time, some black groups fought against each other, and the South African security forces put them down. Shootings, riots, and bombings swept the country. People were afraid, and many wondered if the future would be brighter or if chaos would take over the country. There were many deaths in the four years between Mandela's release and the democratic elections of 1994. Before the dawn, the night was very dark.

A NEW FLAG

With the end of apartheid, a new South African flag was adopted on April 27, 1994. Replacing the old one used since 1928, the flag's colors and shapes symbolized unity. The red, white, and blue were the colors of the historical Boer and British flags. The yellow, black, and green represented the colors of the ANC and other black organizations. The green Y shape showed the unity of the different groups and the movement forward to a new future.

Nobel Peace Prize

The world recognized the great efforts of Mandela and de Klerk to heal the nation. In 1993, the two men received the prestigious Nobel Peace Prize "for their work for the peaceful termination of the apartheid regime, and for laying the foundations for a new democratic South Africa." The Nobel Committee lauded them for looking ahead "instead of back at the deep wounds of the past" and setting an example for the rest of the world. The committee praised their "personal integrity and great political courage."[6]

In his Nobel lecture, de Klerk spoke about the task of bringing peace and reconciliation to South Africa: "The new era which is dawning in our country, beneath the great southern stars, will lift us out of the silent grief of our past and into a future in which there will be opportunity and space for joy and beauty—for real and lasting peace."[7] For Mandela, the award confirmed that the world was rooting for the freedom of his people.

Elections

On April 27, 1994, Mandela cast his vote in the first nonracial South African national elections. He voted at Ohlange High School outside Durban. He chose the polling station because the first president of the ANC, John Dube, one of his heroes, was buried nearby. As he voted, Mandela thought of Dube and the many antiapartheid fighters who had made the day possible. "I did not go into that voting station alone on April 27; I was casting my vote with all of them," he wrote later.[8]

A confident South African President Nelson Mandela smiles for the camera in Bonn, Germany on May 22, 1996, during one of his many world trips.

All across South Africa, some twenty-two million people waited in long lines that wound like snakes to the polls. This marked the first time that most of them were allowed to vote in their own country's election. For a few days, South Africa was quiet. The violence and bombings had ceased. Despite rumors of fraud and missing ballots, the election went smoothly, and people accepted the results.

The ANC won 62.6 percent of the vote, not quite the two-thirds needed for a complete victory. To draft a new constitution, the ANC needed the support of the other political parties. A "national unity" government was formed with the National Party and the Zulus' Inkatha Freedom Party. In other words, compromise was required. "I saw my mission as one of preaching reconciliation, of binding the wounds of the country, of engendering trust and confidence," Mandela wrote.[9] De Klerk, in a speech of concession, lauded him. "Mandela has walked a long road, and now stands at the top of the hill … As he contemplates the next hill, I hold out my hand to Mr. Mandela—in friendship and in cooperation," said de Klerk.[10]

The core of the new constitution was equality. Similar to the US Constitution, it addressed democracy, responsibility, and freedom. The constitution also guaranteed specific rights to education; housing; the ability to strike; freedom of information; equal rights for women, gays, and children; and protection of the environment. The document promised that even if the rights were not achieved immediately, the government must show that it was moving toward that goal.

South Africa's new constitution and democratically elected government ended three centuries of oppression and legalized inequality. The racist government of apartheid was finally put out to sea. Majority rule, rather than white supremacy, was the law of the land. Yet while the changes were historic and significant, the white minority still held economic power, even while blacks gained overwhelming political power. This perilous combination was a recipe for instability for years come.

Inauguration

Stability was also important to a country that had been in turmoil for so long. South Africa needed a leader who could heal old wounds and not break open new ones. The leader would also have to stand on the world stage. South Africa had been cut off from the international community because of its apartheid government. Trade, sports, cultural exchanges, and even tourism had come to a halt. The new leader would need to prove that a new era had begun. He would have to be a peacemaker and goodwill ambassador. No one was as fit for the job as Mandela.

As leader of the victorious ANC party, Mandela was inaugurated the first black president of South Africa on May 10, 1994, in the Union Buildings in Pretoria. De Klerk was made his first deputy. Mandela's longtime comrade in the ANC, Thabo Mbeki, was the second in command in the new Government of National Unity. In his inaugural speech, Mandela thanked the masses of people, the youth, women, and others, as well as de Klerk, who contributed to this special day. He said, "The time for the healing of the wounds has come. The moment to bridge the chasms that divide us has come. The time to build is upon us. We have, at last, achieved our political emancipation." He also noted that there "is no easy road to freedom."[11]

"We must therefore act together as a united people, for national reconciliation, for nation building, for the birth of a new world. Let there be justice for all. Let there be peace for all. Let there be work, bread, water and salt for all. Never, never and never again shall it be that this beautiful land will again experience the oppression of one by another and suffer the indignity of being the skunk of the world. Let freedom reign. God bless Africa."[12]

9

Truth and Reconciliation

I n 1995, the Rugby World Cup came to Johannesburg. No longer banned from international sports, South Africa was eager to compete again. Even better, the national rugby team, the Springboks, had made it to the finals. The last game, set for June 24, 1995, would be a momentous event for rugby fans, but would the majority of South Africans turn on their TVs or even care?

Rugby, a rough game of strength and speed, was considered an Afrikaner sport. Few blacks played rugby or attended games, preferring the game of soccer. To many blacks, the Springboks, made up of Afrikaner athletes except for one coloured player, symbolized the bleak days of apartheid when only whites were allowed on the sports fields. But Mandela saw the Rugby World Cup as an opportunity for unity. The former boxer knew that people forget their differences on sports fields and in the viewing stands. He made sure to be at the game. "Sport has the power to change the world. It has the power to inspire, it has the power to unite people in a way that little else does. It speaks to youth in a language they understand," he said later.[1]

Mandela wore a green-and-gold No. 6 Springboks jersey. He cheered in the stands at Ellis Park Stadium as the game unfolded. Following his example, around

Nelson Mandela raises his hand to take the oath of office during his inauguration as the new president of South Africa on May 10, 1994, at the Union Building in Pretoria.

the country, blacks and whites kept track of the game. The score was close, and the players worked hard. South Africa won by a score of 15 to 12.

After the victory, Mandela walked onto the field to hand the team captain, Francois Pienaar, the trophy. Later, both men acknowledged what had been said: "Francois, thank you for what you have done for our country." Pienaar replied: "No, Mr. President, thank you for what you have done for our country."[2] Cameras snapped, and the image of friendship between the black president and the Afrikaner rugby star was broadcast around the world. The crowd of Afrikaners, Mandela's former enemies, rose to their feet, cheering for the president. "Nelson! Nelson!" they shouted. In the streets, people of all races erupted with joy at the Springboks' victory. For one day, at least, Mandela's dream of a unified nation had materialized.

Truth and Reconciliation Commission

Sports were not the only way to heal a nation. Mandela believed South Africa should not bury its past, but rather confront the violence and abuses of apartheid. The Truth and Reconciliation Commission (TRC) was established to accomplish this monumental task. Courts were set up to gather testimony from victims, witnesses, and perpetrators. Victims provided details of the violence inflicted on them during apartheid. They were eligible for reparations and rehabilitation. Perpetrators could request amnesty if their actions were motivated by political beliefs. Some 21,000 victims applied to the program, and 2,000 testified at public hearings. The commission also received 7,112 applications for amnesty and granted amnesty to 849 cases.[3]

The promise of "truth for amnesty" for the perpetrators of the abuses was balanced with reparation and rehabilitation for the victims. "We are extricating ourselves from a system that insulted our common humanity by dividing us from one another on the basis of race and setting us against each other as oppressed and oppressor. That system committed a crime against humanity," said Mandela.[4] In 2011, the government paid a sum to all victims registered by the TRC. However, some felt that the payment was insufficient and that more had to be done. Some victims were still fighting for adequate reparations in 2016.

Graca Machel

Mandela's wife, Winnie, had been active in the anti-apartheid struggle during his long prison sentence. Her nickname was "the Mother of the Nation." Her political activities had led her to be arrested, detained, and imprisoned in solitary confinement. As president, Mandela appointed her deputy minister of Arts, Culture, and Technology. Yet Winnie was controversial. After the end of apartheid, the TRC determined that she had violated human rights and engaged in other crimes. She turned against the ANC and Mandela. Later, though, she returned to politics and the ANC. In 2009, she was elected to Parliament and was still serving in 2017.

The marriage between Mandela and Winnie did not last. They separated in 1992 and were divorced in 1996. On July 18, 1998, Mandela married Graca Machel in a private ceremony. The day was also his eightieth birthday. Machel was the widow of the president of Mozambique. Born in 1945, she was much younger than Mandela, but they shared a passion for improving the lives of Africans.

With his wife Graca Machel at his side, Mandela waves to the crowds at the closing ceremony of the 2010 FIFA Soccer World Cup on July 11, 2010, at the FNB Stadium in Soweto. This was his last public appearance.

Machel had received honors for her advocacy work for refugees, women, human rights, and sustainable development in Africa. Mandela felt fortunate to have such a close companion in his later years.

Passing the Reins

Mandela spent his time as president easing the nation's transition from apartheid to a multiracial democracy and mending the rifts in South African society. He traveled around the world, gathering support for a unified South Africa. He met presidents and kings and attended conferences where he was the honored speaker. Dozens of awards were handed out to him. He became even more famous and beloved.

But Mandela did not want to serve more than one term. He wanted to encourage democracy and regular elections and to set a good example for future leaders. Five years after he was inaugurated president, Mandela passed the reigns to his deputy president, Thabo Mbeki, in June 1999. Mbeki was a longtime ANC activist who had spent twenty-eight years in exile during the apartheid struggle. Devoted to a resurgent South Africa, he would be reelected to a second term in 2004.

HIV/AIDS Crisis

Mandela retired from public life in 2004. Even out of office, he worked to make his country better. Makgatho Lewanika Mandela was Mandela's son with his first wife, Evelyn Mase. He was an attorney. On January 6, 2005, he died of AIDS-related illness at age fifty-four. Rather than keeping his grief private, the eighty-six-year-old

Mandela chose to use the death as an opportunity to change public attitudes toward HIV and AIDS. "My son has died of AIDS," he told the nation in his grief.[5] He urged families to speak more openly and face the health crisis that was devastating their country. He urged people to see it as a normal illness, not as a curse. "That is the only way of making an ordinary illness ordinary instead of following those who are not well-informed," he said.[6]

For many years, the country had struggled with HIV, a disease of the immune system that leads to AIDS, a chronic and life-threatening condition if left untreated. At that time, more than five million people were infected with HIV, the largest number of any country, and one thousand people a day were dying of complications from AIDS.[7]

Part of the problem was the shame surrounding the disease. People were afraid to talk about it, much less take action to improve treatment. Mandela regretted not doing more to fight AIDS when he was president. Now he urged South Africa to move quickly to address the problem. Unfortunately, South Africa continues to struggle with HIV/AIDS, along with tuberculosis. Some seven million people, or 19 percent of people ages fifteen to forty-nine, were living with HIV in 2016. With better education, testing, and medical outreach, more people are receiving treatment, and the rate of infection is decreasing. Yet, of all nations in the world, South Africa remains hardest hit by HIV/AIDS.[8]

Final Days

In August 2007, a statue of Mandela was unveiled in Trafalgar Square in London. He made the trip, despite health problems, to be there and also attend a conference on poverty. Over fifty years earlier, he had gone to London as a young man to seek support for the ANC. Now he was returning as an international icon of peace. The last public glimpse of Mandela was at the closing of the 2010 World Cup soccer tournament at the FNB Stadium near Soweto in Johannesburg. The ninety-one-year-old Mandela wore a winter coat and a fur hat as he and his wife waved to the cheering, standing crowds.

MANDELA'S CHILDREN AND GRANDCHILDREN

Mandela was married three times, to Evelyn, Winnie, and Graca. He had six children: four girls and two boys. His daughter Makaziwe died as an infant in 1948. His son Madiba Thembekile (Thembi) died in a car accident in 1969. Another son, Makgatho Lewanika, died of an AIDS-related illness in 2005. His daughters Pumla Makaziwe (Maki), Zenani, and Zindziswa (Zindzi) survived him. In 2015, Mandela had eighteen grandchildren and seventeen great-grandchildren. One of his grandsons, Ndaba Mandela, has "carried the torch" of his grandfather and works on issues such as vaccinations, AIDS education, and economic investment in South Africa.

For many years, Mandela had suffered from poor health and was in and out of hospitals. He'd been treated for prostate cancer and lung problems. His final days were spent surrounded by love. His daughter Makaziwe Mandela later told the BBC, "Until the last moment he had us, you know … The children were there, the grandchildren were there, Graca was there, so we are always around him and even at the last moment, we were sitting with him on Thursday the whole day."[9] All the world held its breath, hoping he would live longer. No one could imagine South Africa without the father of the nation.

On December 5, 2013, Mandela died from a lung infection at age ninety-five. He died peacefully in his home in a Johannesburg suburb. South Africa's president, Jacob Zuma, announced the news to a devastated nation.

The news swept around the world, and mourning mixed with adulation and tributes. Former US president Bill Clinton tweeted, "I will never forget my friend Madiba."[10] F. W. de Klerk said, "Tata, we shall miss you, but know that your spirit and example will always be there to guide us to the vision of a better and more just South Africa."[11] US president Barack Obama called him "a giant of history, who moved a nation toward justice, and in the process moved billions around the world."[12] Even the Empire State Building was lit with the colors of the South African flag for two nights in honor of Mandela.

A national memorial service was held at the FNB Stadium. Some ninety-five thousand people filled the seats. Many wore the colors of the ANC. Thousands more viewed the events on large screens in three other stadiums. Along with the tens of thousands of South Africans were many world leaders, including then US president Barack Obama, President François Hollande of France, and

Prime Minister David Cameron of the United Kingdom, as well as leaders from Brazil, Palestine, India, and other nations. Former US presidents George W. Bush; Bill Clinton and his wife, Hillary; and Jimmy Carter also attended. Rock stars Peter Gabriel and Bono were also there. Mandela's wife, Graca, and his former wife Winnie embraced each other.

Rain fell on the stadium as speakers took turns at the microphone. Obama, who like Mandela was the first black president of his country, spoke to the crowd. "While I will always fall short of Madiba's example, he makes me want to be better. He speaks to what is best inside us. After this great liberator is laid to rest; when we have returned to our cities and villages, and rejoined our daily routines, let us search then for his strength—for his largeness of spirit—somewhere inside ourselves."[13]

> **"Madiba is looking down on us. There is no doubt he is smiling and he watches his beloved country, men and women, unite to celebrate his life and legacy."—Andrew Mlangeni, a former prisoner on Robben Island with Mandela, speaking at the Nelson Mandela memorial.[14]**

From December 11 to December 13, Mandela's body lay in state in the Union Buildings in Pretoria. Mourners lined up to pay their respects. The Union Buildings symbolized the long years of apartheid. Mandela was sworn in as president on the steps. Now the buildings were the center of government for a free and democratic South Africa. Some two thousand people an hour filed past to catch one last glimpse of Madiba.

With a rousing speech of celebration and grief, US President Barack Obama bids farewell to Mandela at the public memorial service at the FNB stadium in Johannesburg, on December 10, 2013.

On his final journey, Mandela's coffin was flown to his childhood home of Qunu in Eastern Cape Province for burial. The roads were lined with people. On December 15, his funeral and burial took place in Qunu. The funeral was attended by some forty-five hundred people. Some were dressed in traditional tribal clothes, and others in dark suits. During a four-hour memorial service, South African president Zuma read a statement that Mandela had spoken at the Rivonia Trial: "I hate race discrimination most intensely and in all its manifestations. I have fought it all my life. I fight it now and will do so until the end of my days."[15] Mandela's granddaughter Nandi Mandela described how Mandela had walked barefoot to school and went on to become president. "It is to each of us to achieve anything you want in life," she said of his message. In the Xhosa language, Nandi Mandela added, "Go well, Madiba, go well to the land of our ancestors, you have run your race."[16] South African Air Force jets flew overhead while soldiers gave a twenty-one-gun salute, and a trumpeter played a song of mourning as Mandela was lowered into the ground.

CONCLUSION

At Mandela's funeral, Ngangomhlaba Matanzima, a Thembu chief who was his nephew, said sadly, "A great tree has fallen."[1] Especially in South Africa, the loss was felt as if Mandela were a member of everyone's own family. It seemed impossible that he was gone. A great moral and political leader, whose life and work had moved the world closer to justice, Mandela was also known for his warmth and sense of humor. Many called him Tata, the Xhosa word for "father."

Born in a small village to parents who couldn't read or write, Mandela became a lawyer, a revolutionary, a prisoner for twenty-seven years, and South Africa's first black president. He enjoyed great successes and endured suffering and deprivation. Fueled by a mixture of idealism and pragmatism, Mandela was willing to pay any price for his goal of freedom and justice for South Africans.

Mandela did not defeat apartheid on his own. Tens of thousands of people gave their lives to bring dignity and justice to South Africans. In the end, South Africa's former president F. W. de Klerk and others in government also worked to release Mandela from prison and negotiate the transition of South Africa into a democracy. Together, they created a country where people could make their own choices about whom to marry, where to live, and what school to attend or bus to take. People's race no longer determined their freedom or their future.

Mandela was not uncontroversial. He struggled with moral issues like many people. As the apartheid system tightened its vice, Mandela came to believe that force, in the form of sabotage and not directed at people, was sometimes justified. He was criticized for taking up arms and was considered a terrorist by many, including the United States. Some people believe that apartheid might not have ended without the ANC's turn to violence. Others disagree and wonder if the violence marred the legacy of Mandela and the ANC.

Mandela also knew when to hold out his hand in peace. After his release from prison, he urged forgiveness, rather than vengeance. He wanted a unified country where people treated each other as they would like to be treated themselves. One of his strongest qualities was his concern for others. Mandela wrote, "For to be free is not merely to cast off one's chains, but to live in a way that respects and enhances the freedom of others."[2]

With apartheid gone, the challenges for South Africa were many. As the twenty-first century unfolded, the country contended with the HIV/AIDS epidemic, the poverty of millions of South Africans, and a government often in turmoil. Segregation was no longer the law, but true equality of opportunity, employment, and welfare would take time to achieve. Many blacks continued to struggle in crowded townships with little opportunity for a better life. The economic divide between white and black would take longer to erase than the attitudes and laws that had created the inequities decades ago. Yet South Africa was also a nation full of possibilities—a rainbow nation with a strong democratic constitution, nine provinces and eleven different official languages representing its many diverse peoples, and a wellspring of hope for the future.

During his long life, Mandela was a fighter and a peacemaker, a revolutionary and a world dignitary. He filled all those shoes and kept on walking. The last words in Mandela's autobiography, *Long Walk to Freedom*, describe a man who is restless and knows that the struggle for full human dignity and political freedom is never finished. More work can always be done. Holding his gaze on the future, Mandela was filled with both hope and trepidation. He wrote that the journey to freedom for the South African people was not over and that more work was required. "I have discovered the secret that after climbing a great hill, one only finds that there are many more hills to climb," he wrote. He wrote that even though he may take a moment to rest and enjoy the views, he cannot stop for long: "I dare not linger, for my long walk is not ended."[3]

CHRONOLOGY

1910 The Union of South Africa is formed by former British colonies and Boer republics; racial segregation becomes official policy.

1912 The South African Native National Congress, later renamed the African National Congress (ANC), is founded to give blacks a political voice in South Africa.

1913 The Natives Land Act restricts ownership of land for South Africa's blacks.

1918 Rolihlahla Mandela is born on July 18 in the Transkei.

1925 Mandela enters primary school near Qunu; his teacher gives him the name Nelson.

1930 After his father dies, Mandela is cared for by the regent of the Thembu people; he lives in Mqhekezweni at the Great Place.

1934 Mandela is initiated into manhood with the traditional circumcision ritual; he attends boarding school in Engcobo.

1937 Mandela starts classes at the South African Native College, the only black university in South Africa, and meets Oliver Tambo.

1940 Mandela is expelled from Fort Hare for protesting.

1941 Mandela runs away to Johannesburg and works in the gold mines; Walter Sisulu finds him work as a clerk in a law office.

1942 Mandela begins attending ANC meetings.

1943 Mandela graduates with a BA from the University of South Africa (by correspondence) and starts law studies at the University of Witwatersrand.

1944 Mandela cofounds the ANC Youth League and marries Evelyn Ntoko Mase.

1948 The National Party wins general election; Parliament passes laws to establish apartheid.

1950 The Population Registration Act classifies people according to race.

1952 The ANC starts the Defiance Campaign with the Day of Protest on June 26; Mandela is arrested several times; he is convicted under the Suppression of Communism Act and sentenced to nine months of hard labor, suspended for two years, and receives first banning order preventing him from participating in political activity; Mandela and Oliver Tambo open the first black law firm in South Africa.

1953 The Bantu Education Act enforces segregated education in South Africa.

1956 Mandela is arrested on December 5 and charged with high treason against the state. The Treason Trial lasts more than four years; he is found not guilty in 1961.

1958 After divorcing his wife, Mandela marries Nomzamo Winifred Madikizela, a social worker.

1960 Police fire on people protesting the pass laws in the Sharpeville Massacre on March 21; the government declares a state of emergency

and detains Mandela; the ANC and Pan-
Africanist Congress are banned.

1961   Mandela goes underground; the armed wing
of the ANC is formed with Mandela as first
commander in chief; a series of explosions is
set off on December 16.

1962   Mandela leaves South Africa for guerrilla
training; he visits other African states and
London to gain support for the ANC; on
August 5, he is arrested and, in November,
is sentenced to five years for leaving the
country without a passport and inciting
workers to strike.

1963   Mandela is transferred to Robben Island in
May and then to Pretoria Central Prison; he
is put on trial in October for sabotage with
nine others in the Rivonia Trial.

1964   Mandela is sentenced in June to life in prison
and is taken to Robben Island.

1968   Mandela's mother dies; he cannot attend
the funeral.

1969   Mandela's eldest son, Madiba Thembekile
(Thembi), is killed in a car accident.

1976   During the Soweto Uprising on June 16, ten
thousand young people take to the streets
of Soweto to protest being forced to study
Afrikaans; hundreds are massacred by
the police.

1982   Mandela is moved to Pollsmoor Prison in
Cape Town.

1985   Mandela refuses President P. W. Botha's

offer to release him if he renounces violence; he undergoes prostate surgery; he starts talks with members of government about negotiating with the ANC.

1988   A concert to celebrate Mandela's seventieth birthday is held in Wembley Stadium in London; Mandela falls ill with tuberculosis and is moved to Victor Verster Prison near Paarl.

1989   Mandela graduates with a law degree from the University of South Africa.

1990   South Africa lifts the ban on the ANC on February 2; Mandela is released from prison on February 11.

1991   Mandela is elected president of the ANC; the Convention for a Democratic South Africa starts in December.

1993   Mandela and former South African president F. W. de Klerk are awarded the Nobel Peace Prize for helping to end apartheid in South Africa and building the foundations for democracy in the country.

1994   Mandela votes in South Africa's first democratic elections on April 27 and is elected the first president of a democratic South Africa on May 9; his autobiography, *Long Walk to Freedom*, is published.

1996   Mandela divorces his wife, Winnie Mandela.

1998   On his eightieth birthday, Mandela marries Graca Machel on July 18.

1999   After one term as president, Mandela ends his political career.

2001   Mandela is diagnosed with prostate cancer.

2004   Mandela retires from public life.

2005   Mandela's son Makgatho Lewanika Mandela dies from an HIV/AIDS-related illness.

2008   Mandela turns ninety and asks people to continue to fight for social justice.

2009   The United Nations declares Mandela's birthday—July 18—International Nelson Mandela Day.

2013   Mandela dies on December 5 in Johannesburg at age ninety-five; he is buried in his home village of Qunu.

CHAPTER NOTES

Introduction

1. Nelson Mandela, *Long Walk to Freedom* (New York, NY: Back Bay Books/Little, Brown and Company, 1995), p. 363.

2. Mandela, *Long Walk to Freedom*, p. 364.

3. Mandela, *Long Walk to Freedom*, p. 368.

Chapter 1: Son of Royalty

1. Nelson Mandela, *Long Walk to Freedom* (New York, NY: Back Bay Books/Little, Brown and Company, 1995), p. 6.

2. "The Natives Land Act of 1913," *South African History Online*, http://www.sahistory.org.za/topic/natives -land-act-1913.

3. "I Am Prepared to Die," *Nelson Mandela Foundation*, http://db.nelsonmandela.org/speeches/pub_view .asp?pg=item&ItemID=NMS010&txtstr=The%20 names%20of%20Dingane%20and.

4. Mandela, *Long Walk to Freedom*, pp. 13–14.

5. Anthony Sampson, *Mandela: The Authorized Biography* (New York, NY: Vintage Books, 2000), p. 15.

6. Mandela, *Long Walk to Freedom*, p. 28.

7. Sampson, *Mandela*, p. 23.

Chapter 2: Cradle of Humankind

1. Erin Wayman, "Mrs. Ples: A Hominid with an Identity Crisis," *Smithsonian*, April 9, 2012, http://www.smithsonianmag.com/science -nature/mrs-ples-a-hominid-with-an-identity -crisis-59680909.

2. Leonard Thompson, *A History of South Africa* (New Haven, CT: Yale University Press, 2000), p. 36.

3. Robert I. Rotberg, *The Founder: Cecil Rhodes and the Pursuit of Power* (New York, NY: Oxford University Press, 1988), p. 49.

4. "1877. Cecil Rhodes: Confession of Faith," *University of Oregon*, http://pages.uoregon.edu/kimball/Rhodes -Confession.htm.

5. Thompson, *A History of South Africa*, pp. 152–153.

6. "Apartheid Legislation 1850s–1970s," *South African History Online*, http://www.sahistory.org.za/article /apartheid-legislation-1850s-1970s.

7. E. S. Reddy, "Hundred Years of Resistance," *Hindu*, January 29, 2012, http://www.thehindu.com/todays -paper/tp-features/tp-sundaymagazine/hundred -years-of-resistance/article2841366.ece.

8. "Gandhi Explains Satyagraha," *South Africa History Online*, http://www.sahistory.org.za/archive/44 -gandhi-explains-satyagraha.

Chapter 3: City of Gold

1. Nelson Mandela, *Long Walk to Freedom* (New York, NY: Back Bay Books/Little, Brown and Company, 1995), p. 58.

2. Anthony Sampson, *Mandela: The Authorized Biography* (New York, NY: Vintage Books, 2000), p. 33.

3. Sampson, *Mandela*, p. 37.

4. Ibid.

5. Mandela, *Long Walk to Freedom*, p. 96.

6. Mandela, *Long Walk to Freedom*, p. 104.

Chapter 4: Freedom Fighter

1. Nelson Mandela, *Long Walk to Freedom* (New York, NY: Back Bay Books/Little, Brown and Company, 1995), p. 111.

2. "Defiance Campaign, 1952," *South Africa History Online*, http://www.sahistory.org.za/topic/defiance-campaign-1952.

3. "Participants in the 1952 Defiance Campaign," *South Africa: Overcoming Apartheid, Building Democracy, Michigan State University*, http://www.overcomingapartheid.msu.edu/image.php?id=65-254-10E.

4. "Defiance Campaign, 1952," *South Africa History Online*.

5. Mandela, *Long Walk to Freedom*, p. 149.

6. Mandela, *Long Walk to Freedom*, p. 153.

7. Mandela, *Long Walk to Freedom*, p. 150.

8. Mandela, *Long Walk to Freedom*, p. 140.

Chapter 5: Spear of the Nation

1. "Treason Trial 1956–1961," *South Africa History Online*, http://www.sahistory.org.za/article/treason-trial-1956-1961.

2. Nelson Mandela, *Long Walk to Freedom* (New York, NY: Back Bay Books/Little, Brown and Company, 1995), p. 267.

3. Nelson Mandela, *The Struggle Is My Life* (London, UK: Pathfinder Press, 2010), p. 184.

4. Mandela, *Long Walk to Freedom*, p. 271.

5. "Manifesto of Umkhonto we Sizwe," *South Africa History Online*, http://www.sahistory.org.za/archive/manifesto-umkhonto-we-sizwe.

6. Mandela, *Long Walk to Freedom*, p. 201.

7. Mandela, *Long Walk to Freedom*, p. 324.

8. Mandela, *Long Walk to Freedom*, p. 326.

Chapter 6: Prisoner #466/64

1. Nelson Mandela, *Long Walk to Freedom* (New York, NY: Back Bay Books/Little, Brown and Company, 1995), p. 364.

2. Mandela, *Long Walk to Freedom*, p. 368.

3. Ibid.

4. "Toward Robben Island: The Rivonia Trial," *Nelson Mandela Foundation*, https://www.nelsonmandela.org/omalley/cis/omalley/OMalleyWeb/03lv02424/04lv03370/05lv03415.htm.

5. "I Am Prepared to Die," *Nelson Mandela Foundation*, https://www.nelsonmandela.org/news/entry/i-am-prepared-to-die.

6. Mandela, *Long Walk to Freedom*, p. 383.

7. Mandela, *Long Walk to Freedom*, 391.

8. "Nelson Mandela International Day," *United Nations*, http://www.un.org/en/events/mandeladay /apartheid.shtml.

9. Nelson Mandela, *Conversations with Myself* (New York, NY: Picador, 2011), p. 142.

10. Sally Williams, "The Making of Mandela: Long Walk to Freedom," *Telegraph* (London), December 7, 2013, http://www.telegraph.co.uk /newsworldnews/nelson-mandela/10494613/The -making-of-Mandela-Long-Walk-to-Freedom.html.

Chapter 7: Uprising

1. Conor Gaffey, "South Africa: What You Need to Know About the Soweto Uprising 40 Years Later," *Newsweek*, June 16, 2016, http://www.newsweek.com/soweto -uprising-hector-pieterson-memorial-471090.

2. Jonathan S. Landay, "In Ronald Reagan Era, Mandela Branded a Terrorist," *McClatchy DC*, December 6, 2013, http://www.mcclatchydc.com/news/nation -world/world/article24760045.html.

3. Warren Murray, "F. W. de Klerk: World Has Lost a Great Unifier with Nelson Mandela's Death," *Guardian*, December 5, 2013, https://www. theguardian.com/world/2013/dec/06/fw-de -klerk-nelson-mandela-death.

4. Ibid.

Chapter 8: Freedom and Democracy

1. Nelson Mandela, *Long Walk to Freedom* (New York, NY: Back Bay Books/Little, Brown and Company, 1995), p. 563.

2. Anthony Sampson, *Mandela: The Authorized Biography* (New York, NY: Vintage Books, 2000), p. 403.

3. Justice Malala, "Mandela Looked His Enemy in the Eye and Held Him Close," *Telegraph*, December 7, 2013, http://www.telegraph.co.uk/news/worldnews /nelson-mandela/10501060/Mandela-looked-his -enemy-in-the-eye-and-held-him-close.html.

4. Richard Stengel, "Nelson Mandela, 1918–2013: Remembering an Icon of Freedom," *Time*, December 5, 2013, http://world.time.com/2013/12/05/nelson -mandela-1918-2013-remembering-an-icon-of-freedom.

5. Malala, "Mandela Looked His Enemy in the Eye and Held Him Close."

6. "The Nobel Peace Prize 1993," *Nobelprize.org*, https:// www.nobelprize.org/nobel_prizes/peace /laureates/1993/press.html.

7. "F. W. de Klerk Nobel Lecture," *Nobleprize.org*, https:// www.nobelprize.org/nobel_prizes/peace /laureates/1993/klerk-lecture_en.html.

8. Mandela, *Long Walk to Freedom*, p. 618.

9. Mandela, *Long Walk to Freedom*, p. 619.

10. Warren Murray, "FW de Klerk: World has Lost a Great Unifier with Nelson Mandela's Death," *The Guardian*, December 5, 2013, https://www .theguardian.com/world/2013/dec/06/fw-de-klerk -nelson-mandela-death.

11. Nelson Mandela, "Inaugural Speech," *University of Pennsylvania-African Studies Center*, http://www .africa.upenn.edu/Articles_Gen/Inaugural _Speech_17984.html.

12. Ibid.

Chapter 9: Truth and Reconciliation

1. Nelson Mandela, *Notes to the Future: Words of Wisdom* (New York, NY: Simon and Schuster, 2012), p. 113.

2. "Hall of Fame 2015 Inductee: Nelson Mandela," *Rugby World Cup*, http://www.rugbyworldcup.com /news/103750.

3. "Truth Commission: South Africa," *United States Institute of Peace*, http://www.usip.org/publications /truth-commission-south-africa.

4. Nelson Mandela, "Statement by Nelson Mandela on Receiving Truth and Reconciliation Commission Report," *South Africa Government*, http://www .mandela.gov.za/mandela_speeches/1998/981029 _trcreport.htm.

5. Craig Timberg, "Mandela Says AIDS Led to Death of Son," *Washington Post*, January 6, 2005, http://www. washingtonpost.com/wp-dyn/articles/A52781 -2005Jan6.html.

6. Ibid.

7. Ibid.

8. "HIV and AIDS Estimates (2015)," *UN AIDS*, http:// www.unaids.org/en/regionscountries/countries /southafrica.

9. "Mandela Death: Daughter Makaziwe Tells of Final Moments," *BBC News*, December 9, 2013, http://www .bbc.com/news/world-africa-25301146.

10. Tom McCarthy and Oliver Laughland, "Nelson Mandela Dies Aged 95," *Guardian*, December 6, 2013, https://www.theguardian.com/world/2013/dec/05 /nelson-mandela-dies-aged-95-live-updates.

11. Warren Murray, "F. W. de Klerk: World Has Lost a Great Unifier with Nelson Mandela's Death," *Guardian*, December 5, 2013, https://www.theguardian.com/world/2013/dec/06/fw-de-klerk-nelson-mandela-death.

12. David Smith, "Barack Obama Lights Up Damp Nelson Mandela Memorial," *Guardian*, December 10, 2013, https://www.theguardian.com/world/2013/dec/10/nelson-mandela-memorial-service-barack-obama.

13. Ibid.

14. "World Leaders Remember Nobel Peace Prize Winner Nelson Mandela," *Justice Matters*, December 14, 2013, https://csjjusticematters.wordpress.com/2013/12/14/world-leaders-remember-nobel-peace-prize-winner-nelson-mandela.

15. Nelson Mandela, *Long Walk to Freedom* (New York, NY: Back Bay Books/Little, Brown and Company, 1995), p. 326.

16. Ian Gallagher et al., "Madiba, We Are Now Burying You," *Telegraph*, December 14, 2013, http://www.dailymail.co.uk/news/article-2523695/Military-honor-guard-escorts-Nelson-Mandelas-casket-final-resting-place-funeral-takes-place-anti-apartheid-leader.html.

Conclusion: A Great Tree Has Fallen

1. Christopher Torchia, "Mandela Buried in Rolling Hills of South Africa," *San Diego Union-Tribune*, December 13, 2013, http://www .sandiegouniontribune.com/sdut-mandelas-remains -transferred-to-air-base-2013dec13-story.html.

2. Nelson Mandela, *Long Walk to Freedom* (New York, NY: Back Bay Books/Little, Brown and Company, 1995), pp. 624–625.

3. Mandela, *Long Walk to Freedom*, p. 625.

GLOSSARY

African National Congress (ANC) A political party, founded in 1912, led by black activists who fought apartheid; it became the ruling party of postapartheid South Africa.

Afrikaans The language, derived from Dutch, spoken by Afrikaners.

Afrikaner South African descendants of Dutch, German, and French Protestant immigrants; also known as Boers.

amandla The Zulu word for "power"; a rallying cry against apartheid with the response *ngawethu!*, meaning "to us."

apartheid An Afrikaner word meaning "apartness"; the government policy promoting racial segregation and economic and political discrimination against nonwhites in South Africa.

Bantu A group of African languages, including Xhosa.

boycott To refuse to buy products, cooperate, or participate as a way of protesting until changes are made.

coloured A person of mixed European and African or Asian ancestry, as defined by the apartheid government.

guerrilla A fighter in an irregular army using surprise raids to attack the enemy.

kaross The traditional garment made of animal skins and worn by Xhosa chiefs.

kraal A group of huts, fields, and animal pens for a family in rural African villages.

National Party The political party led by Afrikaners that governed South Africa during the apartheid era, from 1948 to 1991.

oppress To treat people in an unfair and cruel way.

pass laws An internal passport system designed to segregate and limit movements of nonwhite South Africans.

Robben Island A small island in Table Bay near Cape Town, home to the prison where Mandela and other antiapartheid activists were confined.

sabotage To deliberately destroy or damage the property of others for a political purpose.

township A residential area for nonwhites, often with substandard housing and services.

Truth and Reconciliation Commission (TRC) The court set up by South Africa in 1995 to uncover the truths of human rights violations during apartheid.

Xhosa A major South African ethnic group made up of many tribes; also one of eleven official South African languages.

Youth League The branch of the ANC that brought Mandela and other young activists into the freedom movement.

FURTHER READING

Books

Broun, Kenneth S. *Saving Nelson Mandela: The Rivonia Trial and the Fate of South Africa.* New York, NY: Oxford University Press, 2012.

Deddenberg, Barry. *Nelson Mandela: "No Easy Walk to Freedom."* New York, NY: Scholastic, 2015.

Gormley, Beatrice. *Nelson Mandela: South African Revolutionary.* New York, NY: Aladdin Books, 2016.

Mandela, Nelson. *Notes to the Future: Words of Wisdom.* New York, NY: Atria Books, 2012.

Paton, Alan. *Cry, the Beloved Country.* New York, NY: Scribner, 2003.

Websites

Apartheid Museum
www.apartheidmuseum.org
The Apartheid Museum in Johannesburg explores the state-sanctioned system of racism and the struggle to end the discrimination against the majority of South Africa's population.

Nelson Mandela Centre of Memory
archive.nelsonmandela.org/home
This website provides an in-depth digital archive of Nelson Mandela's life and times and continues to update the archive regularly with new material.

Nelson Mandela Foundation
www.nelsonmandela.org
The nonprofit foundation founded by Nelson Mandela works for freedom and equality for all people and provides information on his life and achievements.

South Africa History Online
www.sahistory.org.za
This website of South African's history and heritage is run by a nonprofit people's history institution.

Films

Invictus, 2009
Following the end of apartheid, Nelson Mandela and the captain of South Africa's national rugby union team pulled the country together for the 1995 Rugby World Cup final in Johannesburg.

Mandela: Long Walk to Freedom, 2013
This film tells the story of Nelson Mandela's life, from his childhood to his inauguration as the first black president of South Africa.

INDEX